SCHOLASTIC

Understanding
Special Education

A Helpful Handbook for Classroom Teachers

by Cynthia M. Stowe

NEW YORK • TORONTO • LONDON • AUCKLAND • SYDNEY
MEXICO CITY • NEW DELHI • HONG KONG • BUENOS AIRES

Teaching *Resources*

Dedication

*For the generous people
who contributed their moving
stories to this book.*

. . . .

For Nancy and Lindy.

. . . .

And for Robert, always.

Cover design by Adana Jiménez
Interior design by Sydney Wright
ISBN: 0-439-56037-3

Contents

About This Book

In the past, most students with special needs received instruction from specialists outside of the regular classroom. Eventually, these specialists realized this was isolating, however, and came to believe that consistent interaction between kids with "special" needs and "regular" needs was important. They argued that effective instruction could be provided for all kids in the regular classroom. Professionals such as special education teachers, speech therapists, and occupational therapists could be brought into the classroom. Some instruction might need to be provided in a separate space, but kids with special needs could spend most, if not all, of their school days with their peers. This would not only be good for them, but would also offer a wonderful opportunity for all kids to get to know one another.

This book is a resource for you, the classroom teacher, as you work in this inclusion model. Section One provides information about the wide diversity of students you will meet in your classroom. It lists the types of challenges that students with special needs may face. Major challenges are defined, and the unique characteristics of students with each challenge are listed. Then, suggestions for what these students need from you are provided.

Section Two offers information about the special education system that serves students with special needs. This section is organized around questions that are uniquely important to classroom teachers. The appendix on pages 125–128 lists books and Web sites for further exploration of both the challenges that students with special needs face and special education in general.

About Inclusion

A great revolution occurred in 1975 when Congress passed Public Law 94-142, the law that created special education. Suddenly, children with special needs were given the legal guarantee of a free and appropriate education.

As teachers began working with these kids, they realized that most of the children did not need to be placed in isolated special education classrooms; most could learn very happily and successfully in regular classrooms. In addition, if offered special services and instruction in their neighborhood schools, the children had more opportunities for extra-curricular and after-school activities. Not only did the children with special needs flourish, but the other kids in their classrooms got to know and appreciate them.

The advantages of including students with special needs in regular classrooms became so apparent that the Individuals With Disabilities Education Act (IDEA), a 1997 update of Public Law 94-142, stated that these children should receive services and instruction in the "least restrictive environment" possible for each of them. The least restrictive environment is usually the regular classroom. This approach is called the inclusion model. Now let's look at one inclusive classroom.

It's 9:30 in the morning, and Janet Anzovino's fifth-grade class is working independently on their writing projects. Most of the kids are writing stories about an animal that has one magical power. Janet walks over to see how Alice is doing. Alice has attention deficit disorder (ADD), and sometimes she has difficulty getting started with writing projects. Alice is staring into space, holding her pencil at eye height.

Janet says, "Alice, may I read what you wrote yesterday?"

Alice looks up, surprised.

"Your cat has the power to open any door she wants, right?"

Alice nods. "Yesterday, my cat opened all the doors at the bank and then got into the bank vault. But then my cat was pretty bored in there."

"She might want to reconsider what doors she wants to open."

"She's already opened all the food doors, but like she could open pet store doors and let the animals out and . . ."

Janet leaves Alice to her writing.

Andrew, a boy with Down Syndrome, is working in the back of the room with the occupational therapist on his cursive writing skills. Janet notices that his friend Richita turns and smiles at him as he silently forms the letter *a* in the air. After Andrew finishes practicing with his cursive, he will organize a card deck, putting verbs in one pile and nouns in the other, for the class to use later to play a grammar game.

· Janet asks Maria to come to her desk. Maria loves to write, and she is learning to write dialogue. After their conference, Janet suddenly hears a notebook being thrown on the floor. Before she can reach Tomas, her student who suffers from an anxiety disorder, Tomas's desk neighbor Patty, has picked up the notebook and is handing it to him. Tomas gets up from his seat and walks over to the quiet corner in the back of the room where a room divider offers some privacy.

Janet walks over and asks Tomas if he's okay. He nods. "Come back to your desk when you're ready," Janet says.

This is a typical morning in Janet's class, and there certainly were significant challenges. Janet needed to help Alice, her student with ADD begin writing, and just telling Alice "to get to work," was going to be ineffective. Fortunately, Janet understands that the best way to help students with ADD focus on something is to engage their interest. Janet got Alice interested in her story again.

Andrew, the boy with Down Syndrome, needs specific instruction, so having an occupational therapist come into the classroom provided this. Andrew benefits from playing a valued role in the class community. Categorizing nouns and verbs into two separate card decks not only reinforces concepts he needs to know, but also helps him do something that the whole class will appreciate.

The incident with Tomas might have been very disruptive if Janet and other students had reacted with dismay. Tomas threw his notebook because he was frustrated and unable to handle the anxiety his frustration created. This is unacceptable behavior in the classroom. But Janet and his fellow students reacted with calmness. Patty silently handed him his notebook, and Tomas silently went to a quiet area. Janet checked in with him to let him know that she was aware of what had happened and that he could rejoin the class when he was ready. On this morning, Janet's classroom ran smoothly. All the kids were engaged in productive activities, and, best of all, everyone was helping everyone else. Janet had created an atmosphere of openness and acceptance that allowed everyone to be their best.

There are, however, probably days when things don't run as well. Creating and maintaining this level of effectiveness can be challenging within the inclusion model. A teacher may need to modify homework assignments or create additional instructional materials. Having enough support systems built in, such as paraprofessional time or help from the special education teacher or other specialists, is important. If you are feeling overwhelmed by the time and attention needed by your student with special needs, ask the special education team for help. You will feel better if you feel you're meeting the needs of all the children in your class.

A second challenge for teachers is the worry that giving accommodations and special help to kids with special needs is unfair to the other kids. If a student with a learning disability is allowed to take an oral test in history, for example, why do all the other kids have to take written ones? In this case, it is important to think about the basic issue of fairness. Does being fair mean teaching everyone in exactly the same way? Let's be ridiculous for a moment: Would it be fair to deny a child with a physical disability a wheelchair because the other kids don't need one? The answer here is simple: of course not.

The issue becomes cloudier, however, when a student has a less physically observable challenge. Think of a girl who has difficulty paying attention to one speaker (perhaps the teacher) when surrounded by a roomful of busy and happy students. This student may have ADD and may need her teacher to approach her and to privately tell her the directions for the upcoming assignment. Is this special attention fair? Of course. She needs it. Perhaps the definition of fair needs to become: That which helps each student achieve his or her potential.

A third challenge is how to help all students to be appreciative and respectful of one another. Some kids with special needs may look and/or act differently, which can lead to teasing. How do you handle this, especially when you cannot discuss the special needs or the diagnosis of your student?

Deal with the teasing of kids with special needs and teasing by kids with special needs in the same way you deal with all issues of teasing—with directness. Ask the students involved to come to a safe, private place and discuss the behaviors that you have observed. Hold students accountable for their behaviors. Make it clear that ridicule is not tolerated in your classroom. If you are uncomfortable for any reason, ask for advice and help from your special education team.

Many challenges arise in a classroom where kids with diverse needs and learning styles interact. Is the inclusion model perfect? Probably not. You have real help, however. You are a member of a team that includes the school psychologist, occupational therapist, speech therapist, and school counselor. If you have any problems you feel unable to solve, or if you have any nagging concerns, these are the people to go to. It is a part of their job to assist you as you work and to give you the information you need to help you meet the challenges of your students. An important part of the team's job is to help you from the day your student enters your classroom until the day he or she waves good-bye for summer vacation.

One other thing that is extremely useful as you work with kids with special needs is to read his or her Individual Education Plan (IEP). Every student with special needs has one of these plans, which defines goals and objectives for instruction. The specialists who will provide services write the IEP and provide this instruction. It is helpful for you to read the plan, however, because it tells you approximately at what level your student is functioning. For example, John Hoff's third-grade student Rachel has a reading goal of learning all the sounds of the letters of the alphabet. This informs him that he needs to find picture books with little text or, even better, wordless books for Rachel for silent reading times. It also tells him to be alert to the many opportunities for reinforcing her learning of the alphabet.

There is more specific information about IEPs at the end of this book on pages 115–123.

General Principles
of Working With Students
With Special Needs

There are many things you can do that will significantly help your students with special needs. The following suggestions are offered as guidelines. Some may be obvious. They serve as reminders of how much you are already doing daily in your classroom.

The first and most important thing to remember is that kids with special needs are *kids*. They may have unusual challenges in their lives, but they have the same needs as other children—to be part of the group, to have friends, to play, to feel successful. Understanding and providing special care for their challenges is important, but remembering they are kids comes first.

Students with special challenges in their lives need personal caring from their teacher. Sometimes, this is easy to do. If a student exhibits behaviors that are less than attractive, however, it can be difficult. If you find it difficult to like and enjoy a particular student, first acknowledge the feeling. Then, make an effort to separate your perception of your student from your perception of her behavior. Act in a kind and sympathetic way. Say things like, "I can see that you are having a really hard time sitting still today. What can I do to help you get to work?" She may have a really good idea, and your sensitive reaching out may be just what she needs to get going.

Students with special needs benefit from having clear, reasonable, and consistent expectations to meet. If you are unsure of what to expect from your student in an academic situation (such as weekly spelling tests) or a nonacademic situation (such as when she is out at recess), discuss this with the special education team and create appropriate expectations. Then, make sure that your student is aware of these expectations. Lastly, stick to them. Changing expectations from day to day will only confuse your student and the other students in your class. Confusion often leads to discomfort and feelings of insecurity. Remain open to creative ways to solve problems. There is no one right way to solve a problem.

Be on the lookout for areas in which your student performs well and point this out to her. Some words of praise for a true success encourage further hard work and dedication.

Try to find a talent or strength in your student and give her opportunities to utilize it. Does your student with severe reading difficulties have a particular talent in art? See if she'd like to design the set for your next class play. Find a job for your student, whether it is helping to care for a classroom pet or organizing part of an activity area. Everyone profits from having something to contribute to the classroom.

All students deserve privacy. Be very aware of respecting this privacy. For example, if your student needs to go to the school nurse to get medication every day, be sure this happens in a discreet way.

Be very aware of confidentiality. This is not only the right thing to do, it is also the federal law. You may speak about your student's diagnosis or special needs only to those school professionals, including teachers, who legitimately need to know in order to provide appropriate education to your student. Your school should supply guidelines. You need a signed release form from a parent or guardian to speak with anyone else. For example, if your student is seeing a counselor outside of school, you need written permission in order to share information with that counselor. If you absolutely have to tell someone about an accommodation your student requires (such as a physical prop she needs in order to participate in a game), you can tell that person about the student's need for the accommodation, and that is all. You cannot explain further. There are a few exceptions. In a safety or health emergency, you are allowed to give information to an appropriate professional such as a doctor. In general, however, keep the information about your student private. If you are unsure whether or not you should provide information in any given situation, check with your special education team.

Be aware of your own needs. It's important to keep your sense of humor and to remain confident that you are doing the best job you can. You can get not only information but also emotional support from the people on your student's special education team. Discuss issues that arise, especially ones that trouble you or that you are unsure about how to handle. Ask questions. Ask for help. This help will benefit your student as well as you.

In conclusion, the inclusion model is reflective of real life. Your students with "regular" needs and your students with "special" needs will most probably meet and interact with one another as they go through life. If they can have positive experiences together in school, if they can come to see each other as individuals instead of as faceless beings defined by having disabilities or not having disabilities, the experience will affect their behavior throughout their whole lives.

What Are Some Challenges That Students Face?

Learning Disabilities

The term *learning disability* refers to many different types of learning issues that can vary widely in levels of severity. Students with a learning disability have at least average intelligence. They have areas of high functioning and areas of difficulties. Their learning disabilities are not caused by physical problems, such as vision or hearing impairments, or by primary emotional disturbance, and their challenges are not the result of poor schooling.

Researchers currently believe that neurological issues cause learning disabilities. One research team at Yale University, led by Dr. Sally E. Shaywitz, is using functional magnetic resonance imaging (fMRI) technology to show how the brains of people with dyslexia—a language-based learning disability—function differently than the brains of people without dyslexia (Knopf, 2003).

Students with learning disabilities take in information, such as sights or sounds, but may have difficulty understanding or attaching meaning to it. They find it hard to organize information so that it is readily accessible. Retrieving the information from either short- or long-term memory is difficult. In addition, expressing the information, either verbally through speech or writing, or nonverbally may be a problem. Students with learning disabilities often exhibit wide discrepancies between different skill areas; in other words, they may be good readers but may have great problems with spelling. They can have difficulty with listening, speaking, reasoning, reading, writing, spelling, math, motor skills, and social skills. People with learning disabilities tend to be hard workers who have many gifts. But without appropriate instruction, they do not achieve their potential.

In this section, you'll find information on four kinds of learning disabilities:

dyslexia: page 15

dyscalcula: page 22

dysgraphia: page 25

nonverbal learning disability: page 28

Dyslexia

Arthur Granger's second-grade student Emma was a sweet and cooperative child who was having some trouble learning to read. This surprised Arthur because Emma spoke fluently, had an excellent vocabulary, and was doing very well on her weekly spelling tests. It was late October when another student declared that Emma was cheating on a spelling test—she was copying her answers from a list. When Arthur spoke with her privately, Emma tearfully explained that she wasn't cheating, that she just couldn't remember all the words and that she needed her list to do a good job on the test. In spite of practicing every night with her dad, she couldn't remember how to spell the words. Arthur understood that Emma hadn't meant to cheat; she desperately wanted to be successful.

Now it was evident, however, that Emma was having real difficulty with reading and spelling. After speaking with her parents, Arthur referred her for an evaluation. The results indicated that Emma had dyslexia.

What is dyslexia?

Dyslexia is a learning disability that affects a person's ability to deal with, acquire, and process language. It can affect all the academic areas where language is involved: reading, spelling, writing, handwriting, and math. Researchers currently believe dyslexia is an inherited, neurologically based condition. It is not caused by lack of motivation, poor instruction, or other environmental issues. Dyslexia takes many different forms and differs widely in levels of severity. (This definition is adapted from the International Dyslexia Association's definition of dyslexia.)

What are some unique characteristics of students with dyslexia?

Students with dyslexia have average or above average intelligence. A typical dyslexic child is bright and highly creative, with a good sense of humor and the ability to see things in new ways. In his fascinating book *In the Mind's Eye: Visual Thinkers, Gifted People With Dyslexia and Other Learning Difficulties, Computer Images and the Ironies of Creativity* (Prometheus Books,

1997), Thomas G. West talks about how the learning style associated with dyslexia was an advantage when our culture was agrarian. Back then, people had to rely on logical thinking and creative ways to solve problems. Once our society became dependent on skills associated with two-dimensional text (reading and writing), the learning style created problems for people. He speculates that in our "new" world of computers and corporate culture, the learning style will, once again, become advantageous. In his book, West also tells the stories of several famous people who exhibited characteristics of dyslexia and were able to capitalize on their strengths. Among them are inventor Thomas Edison, British prime minister Winston Churchill, and General George Patton.

Myth

Dyslexia is not just about letter and number reversals. Some people with dyslexia do reverse letters and numbers, but lots of children with more typical learning styles do also, especially before the age of seven.

Dyslexia is a different learning style, not an inferior one. It requires different methods of instruction. Often, students with dyslexia need explicit and detailed instruction in:

- understanding the meaning of certain information.
- organizing this data.
- retrieving it from short- or long-term memory.
- expressing this knowledge orally or in writing.

Students with dyslexia often need explicit instruction in phonemic awareness because they have difficulty associating sounds with letters, knowing how many sounds there are in a word, and sequencing the sounds in words. They can see the letters and hear the sounds, but it's hard for them to remember the association between them. Often they are more successful on some days than on others, adding to their frustration. Brian MacDowell thought his third-grade student Nellie finally knew all her letter sounds. On a Wednesday morning, she was so proud when she asked him to test her and she got them all right. The next morning, however, when

Nellie was reading the sentence "Sam went to the store and got a bicycle," she stopped, confused by "bicycle." When Brian suggested that she look at the beginning of the word for a clue as to what Sam might have gotten, she guessed "hat" and then "kitten."

Naturally Brian felt disappointed that Nellie was not able to retain the letter-sound connection for *b*. When he spoke with the special education teacher about this, he learned that because dyslexia is a neurological condition, factors that we are currently unaware of could influence functioning. The important thing is to persevere with the instruction and, eventually, a student like Nellie will be more consistently successful.

Students with dyslexia may also need instruction with auditory discrimination, or hearing the small differences between sounds. They hear the sounds but often can't perceive differences between them. Short vowel sounds are particularly hard.

Students with dyslexia may have difficulty remembering what they hear. Particularly difficult are words or numbers that have little meaning in themselves, such as the days of the week or telephone numbers. In addition, visual memory, or remembering what they see, may pose a problem. They may not remember or recognize spelling words or sight words. This is why students with dyslexia have such difficulty with irregular words. If your mind doesn't take a "visual photograph" after a few exposures to a word and store it in your memory bank, how can you remember how to spell words such as *enough* or *believe*?

Everyone has some visual memory. While some people with highly advanced photographic memories can look at a page of text and immediately recite it back, most of us need a few exposures to individual words or phrases to remember them. People with dyslexia have weak visual memories for text and need lots of exposures to remember words. For irregular words especially, they may need explicit instruction, practice, and review.

Students with dyslexia can have difficulty with both fine motor and gross motor coordination. The former can affect the ability to perform tasks such as handwriting, as well as the speed at which such a task is accomplished. The latter can affect balance.

Difficulty with the organization of time and tasks is another hallmark of dyslexia. It is important for students to have an understanding of how they learn best and how they can use their strengths to approach a job, especially a multistep project, efficiently and effectively. This ability, called *executive function*, may be an area of weakness for students with dyslexia, which makes planning homework and projects very difficult.

The organization of space is also often problematic. Students with dyslexia usually have messy desks and frequently misplace school supplies. Tremont, a seventh grader, once lost his three-ring binder traveling from the study hall to his English class, though the study hall was only two doors away.

In addition to strictly academic issues, students with dyslexia may have challenges with social relationships. They may be immature in physical and social development, maturing eventually, but taking more time than is typical. They may experience a lack of awareness in social situations that is the result of misunderstanding social cues. Being uncomfortable in social situations due to past academic failure and embarrassment in front of peers is also an issue.

In addition to their social discomfort, students with dyslexia can have feelings of insecurity and anger regarding schoolwork because they have experienced failure in the past.

Some students with dyslexia have other learning difficulties. Two common ones are attention deficit disorder (ADD) and attention deficit hyperactivity disorder (ADHD).

What does my student with dyslexia need from me?

Structure and Organization

Students with dyslexia often relax when things are structured and predictable. They benefit from being in a neat, calm, uncluttered classroom. One way to create predictability is to tell your whole class what is going to happen during an upcoming lesson. You can say, for example, "We're going to do creative writing for the next fifty minutes. First, we're all going to talk about our favorite animals and tell interesting stories about them for about ten minutes. Then, we're going to write by ourselves for about thirty minutes. Then, volunteers can share their writing." Even if this is the regular way you do creative writing, it will help your student with dyslexia to know that this is a normal day and this is what he can expect on this particular day. If there are going to be any changes in the day's schedule, tell him ahead of time to prepare him.

If your classroom is very busy, you might want to put up a small room divider or screen that blocks out some of the stimulation for quiet work times. Playing soft music on a tape or CD player during independent work times can be very calming.

And provide pencils. Although it's important to help students learn responsibility, keeping track of pencils is downright impossible for many students with dyslexia. Just make it a nonissue by always having "free" pencils available. Alice Tyler thought this might be a problem in her fifth-grade classroom, so she asked her students to contribute pencils to the pencil jar whenever they could, and only take pencils when absolutely necessary. Occasionally, Alice had to add pencils to the jar, but not very often.

Curriculum

Become familiar with the goals and objectives on your student's IEP. Beth Chadwick's fifth-grade student Henry has a reading goal that says, "Henry will read one-syllable words that have the phonetic pattern: a vowel, a consonant, and a silent *e*." Words like *cake*, *pine*, *home*, and *mule* follow this pattern. Beth is not directly responsible for teaching Henry this pattern in reading, but many opportunities may arise in the classroom that will reinforce his learning. For example, one afternoon when students were settling in from recess, one boy was talking about a funny movie he had seen about a gorilla. Beth casually turned to the chalkboard behind her and said, "Ah, gorillas are a kind of ape. Oh, look at that: The word *ape* follows the pattern that has a vowel, a consonant, and a silent *e*. Look at that: *a*, *p*, and silent *e*. It says *ape*."

Many students with dyslexia have great difficulty with spelling, so weekly class spelling tests may be times of frustration and embarrassment for them. Thomas, an adult with dyslexia, constantly felt humiliated by his difficulties with spelling as a child. He tells the story of his parents coming

> # Myth
>
> Current studies show that dyslexia occurs with equal frequency in girls and in boys. Older studies only counted students who were referred for special services. In the past, boys were referred more frequently for services because of a higher incidence of behavior problems. Also, people tended to have higher academic expectations for boys than for girls.

to an open house in his fourth-grade classroom. There on the bulletin board was a large chart with every child's name. The dates of all the spelling tests were listed, and gold stars were awarded for all the 100s achieved. Thomas says that as he stood there with his mother and father looking at the chart, he realized that he was the only child with no stars next to his name. His heart sank then, and it still sinks now whenever he thinks of that night.

If your student with dyslexia needs to take spelling tests with the rest of the class, speak with the special education teacher about how this situation can be structured for him to be successful. Sometimes, students are asked to write fewer words. Selecting words that follow the same phonetic pattern, such as *rain*, *train*, and *maintain*, is a good strategy.

As much as possible, learn about your student's interests and use these as much as you can in the curriculum. For example, if your student is particularly interested in basketball, use basketball imagery in math, in writing, even in social studies (for example, what games and sports are played in the place being studied?). You may not always be able to do this, but your student will appreciate your effort. Students with dyslexia have a much easier time focusing on a topic that is interesting to them.

Since students with dyslexia often have such difficulty with executive function (knowing how to approach and complete a task), it is important to take an active role in helping your student gain skills in this area. The executive function helps in several ways. It is like a personal manager. It helps a person take in and organize new information, prioritize what needs to be done, plan the steps that need to be taken, and figure out the strategies that should be used to accomplish the task. Finally, it evaluates the effectiveness of the plan. The special education teacher may be providing explicit instruction in this area, but as the classroom teacher, you are in a unique position to monitor how your student is doing and in what areas he needs more help. It is extremely important for your student to learn how to function independently with homework and class assignments, especially as he moves into higher grades. Anything you can do to strengthen his executive function will be a great help.

Expectations

Remember that students with dyslexia often function at different levels on different days. Reena Gonfrad discovered that her fifth-grade student Randy was able to spell certain words and to keep his school supplies in relatively neat order on some days. Other days, he would spell the same words wrong, and his desk would be an absolute mess. Reena realized that Randy's behavior was not the result of laziness or stubbornness. Some days, his circuits just worked better than on other days. On Randy's "off" days, Reena learned to restructure her expectations as much as possible, so that Randy could be successful. Reena also needed to help him know that this fluctuation was a normal part of his learning and that eventually he would function more consistently. Reena's confidence helped Randy relax so that emotional issues did not compound the fluctuations.

Social Relationships With Peers

Model appropriate behavior in social situations. If your student is having a particular problem, such as knowing how to share materials at an art station, find a private time to speak with him and show him explicitly which behaviors and actions are helpful. If he is having numerous difficulties in a wide variety of social situations, keep track of these and speak with the special education teacher about them. Because you see your student in many large group settings, you are a valuable source of helpful information to the special education teacher.

Jake's Story

Jake is a sixth-grade student with dyslexia. He only began receiving appropriate instruction late in fifth grade, so he is a beginning reader. Although he repeatedly said he didn't want to read, he would look at books about heavy equipment such as bulldozers. Jake's teacher found as many books as possible on heavy equipment for him.

After a while, however, the teacher's spirits flagged—she'd been unable to find new books about heavy equipment for Jake. And then it happened. One morning, Jake turned to her and said, "I like these books, but I can read other books, too." The teacher's heart raced. She could barely breathe. Jake continued, "I can read books about the parts in these machines."

Alas, the breakthrough did not occur that day. But several weeks later, Jake talked about seeing a moose cross a road in a small city near where he lived. He started being interested in books about large animals, and then about dogs, and then about insects. (A favorite aunt of his had given him an ant farm for his birthday.) After a few months, he was open to reading about a wide variety of topics.

Dyscalcula

Norman, a student with dyscalcula, was unable to read the analog clock in his fourth-grade classroom. This didn't surprise Sonia Paulson since many other kids had the same difficulty. But when the class was on a field trip and Sonia saw Norman hand the store clerk two dollar bills for a 75¢ souvenir, she realized how much his dyscalcula was affecting him.

Sonia was grateful that Norman was receiving special instruction for mathematics with the special education teacher, but she resolved to find more opportunities for math games in the classroom. She even decided to create a mini "store" with classroom money that all the kids could play with.

Norman loved the store. He told Sonia, "I know that I need help with this. Thank you for making this for me and for the other kids."

What is dyscalcula?

Dyscalcula (or dyscalculia) is a learning disability that affects a person's functioning in mathematics. It can affect abstract reasoning skills in math and/or the ability to perform mathematical computations. Lining up the problems in correct rows and columns can be difficult, and numbers can be reversed. For word problems, it can be difficult knowing which mathematical operations to use. Memorizing math facts can also be difficult (Hammeken, 2000).

What are some unique characteristics of students with dyscalcula?

Students with dyscalcula have difficulty understanding mathematical concepts, such as what numbers mean. They may also be challenged by the reasoning needed for math, such as knowing which mathematical process to use in a given word problem and the appropriate sequence of steps required to solve it.

Computation challenges may include difficulty memorizing math facts, such as addition facts, subtraction facts, and multiplication tables. They may have spatial issues, which affect their ability to place numbers in the correct places, such as in a division problem.

Students with dyscalcula may have difficulty with everyday math, such as telling time on a regular clock, understanding linear and volume measurements, and making change with money.

What does my student with dyscalcula need from me?

Curriculum

The classroom is an invaluable place for helping your student with math, even if she receives her "official" math instruction from a special education teacher. It's invaluable because during the day there are many opportunities to point out real-life math problems and concepts. Here are two examples of things you might say to respond to something that is happening in your classroom:

"How many seashells did Jesse bring in today? Let's count them."

"Please raise your hand if you want to go to the science museum for our field trip. Okay, ten people have raised their hands. Fourteen of you did not. What fraction of our class wants to go to the science museum?"

Keep a sharp eye out for opportunities that are age and skill appropriate, and you'll assist your student's mathematical understanding and interest a great deal.

Check your student's IEP to see what her specific math goals are so you can find ways to reinforce her learning. Tom McDonnell's fifth-grade student Victoria had the math goal "Victoria will be able to distinguish whether she should add or subtract in word problems." One day, Victoria was putting tabs in a three-ring binder to store her worksheets. She had a tab for math and spelling, but she also told Tom that she wanted tabs for writing, social studies, science, and one for just plain fun: to store her doodles. Tom asked her whether or not she needed to add tabs or subtract tabs. This was easy for Victoria since it was so fully based in the physical world. It was good for her, however, to vocalize which operation she would use.

Provide manipulatives for your student to use in solving computation problems. Dried kidney beans are easily stored in a box and are age appropriate even for older students. Tanya Spicer keeps a carved stone box with small round pebbles in it (she got them at a yard sale) for her sixth-grade student Carolyn. The stones are so attractive and sophisticated, Carolyn likes to use them to check her work.

If your student's spatial issues affect computation, experiment with graph papers of different sizes, and clearly outline the boxes where numbers are to be placed. In addition, provide a copy of any computation or word problems for the student at her desk. Copying from the board is just too hard and, unfortunately, a good opportunity to make errors.

Expectations

If your student needs to complete math homework or a math test in your classroom, give her fewer problems or more time. She will have to think carefully about the math facts, about the steps she's supposed to take, and about where she's supposed to place numbers on the page. These thoughts are not automatic, so she will need more time.

Using Calculators

There is an ongoing controversy about allowing students with dyscalcula to use calculators in the classroom. Some people fear that students will become dependent on calculators for doing simple, real-world activities such as making purchases at a store. Students with dyscalcula can learn math facts with appropriate instruction, they argue, and therefore, they should do so.

Other people feel that calculators help students with dyscalcula relax and function much more like other kids in the classroom. Why should they be denied this help?

The compromise position is to teach students the math facts and to allow calculators for checking their answers. You should discuss this issue with your student's special education teacher to decide on a clear and consistent policy.

Dysgraphia

Latoya doodled in the corners of her papers during class discussions, but her sixth-grade teacher Beth Flanagan didn't mind. Latoya was always attentive and could answer questions, which showed that she was paying close attention. And the geometric patterns and other pictures Latoya created were beautiful.

Even though she drew well, however, Latoya had lots of trouble with handwriting. She had dysgraphia. She was learning cursive writing with the special education teacher (she now had mastered half of the lowercase letters), but one of the accommodations on her IEP was for her to be able to use a word processor for written tasks in class.

This worked well until one day a local author came to do a workshop. During a writing activity with the class, the author asked that everyone use a paper and pencil. She stated, "I'm old-fashioned, I know, but magic happens when you have a pencil in your hand."

Latoya tried. As Beth walked by her desk, however, she was shocked to see Latoya's printing: The letters were ill-formed, off the lines and unevenly spaced. Her printing looked like that of a six-year-old. Beth bent down and asked Latoya if she would like to dictate her thoughts to her, that she would be her "pencil." As Latoya nodded and looked up, Beth saw tears in her eyes.

What is dysgraphia?

Dysgraphia is a learning disability that affects a person's handwriting. People with dysgraphia have difficulty forming letters and spacing letters and words evenly on the page. Their pencil grip is often tight, and the experience of writing by hand is uncomfortable (Stevens, 1996).

What are some unique characteristics of students with dysgraphia?

Students with dysgraphia can have difficulty forming individual letters and putting letters together to create words. When printing, they may have wide and varied spaces between letters and little space between words.

They have difficulty placing letters and words on a common baseline. In addition, they may have an uncomfortable and tight pencil grip.

Students with dysgraphia often have an intense dislike of handwriting because it is so physically difficult for them. Also, some students are embarrassed by their poor handwriting.

What does my student with dysgraphia need from me?

Curriculum

Learning cursive writing is the most beneficial thing for a student with dysgraphia. Many people are surprised by this, thinking cursive writing will be even more difficult than printing. But when cursive writing is taught in a multisensory way, with the letters taught in groups of common starting forms, students with dysgraphia can learn to write beautifully and much more easily. The first letter of a word in cursive writing starts on the baseline. The letters in the words are then connected, which eliminates the issue with spacing in words and makes it easier to stay on the baseline.

The most important thing for you to do, therefore, is to advocate that your student with dysgraphia be taught cursive writing. Two recommended cursive handwriting programs are *The Multisensory Teaching Approach: Handwriting Practice Guide* by Margaret Taylor Smith (Educators Publishing Service, 1988) and *Loops and Other Groups, A Kinesthetic Writing System* by Mary Benbow (Therapy Skill Builders, a division of Communication Skill Builders, 1990). Students can begin to learn cursive writing as early as age seven.

There is an excellent keyboarding program that is appropriate as an addition to a good cursive writing program. *Keyboarding Skills* by Diana Hanbury King (Educators Publishing Service, 1986) works so well because it teaches the keyboard based on the alphabet. Students learn *a* and *b* and then *c* and so on. If students are motivated and patient, it's a very effective program.

Be aware of the handwriting goals on your student's IEP. The goal for John Bravlow's fourth-grade student Victor is "to maintain good writing posture." Two objectives are "Victor will keep his feet on the floor when writing," and "Victor will place his paper on a flat surface at a good height, at a 45-degree angle from his body." John knows that he needs to stay aware of Victor's writing posture in the classroom. If he sees him slumping or leaning over his paper, he can go up to Victor and quietly remind him of this issue. John and Victor might also create a nonverbal cueing system for this. And it's really important for John to model good writing posture.

Special Adaptations

Use paper with wide lines. Your student's skill level will determine how wide the lines must be. Sometimes, it helps to darken the baselines. Plastic pencil grips may relieve the physical tension of gripping the pencil. Some of them are designed to help establish correct pencil grip. These plastic grips can be found in many stationery or office supply stores.

Provide a page with all the cursive letters, including the capitals, at your student's desk or in his notebook. Also, ask your student to copy only from near point as opposed to far point (like from the chalkboard). He needs to have a model, close up.

Expectations

Know that the physical act of writing is difficult for your student with dysgraphia, so expect less writing from him, especially when he is learning cursive. Expect him to work as hard as your other students, but not harder.

A Quote From a Student With Dysgraphia

This student has not yet been taught cursive writing by a multisensory approach. This young man draws beautifully with pencil and pen and ink.

"For some reason, when I write, I always grasp the pen too tightly. The muscles in my upper arm get all tight and tired. It's like a workout."

"When I'm drawing, it's different each time, but when I'm writing, it's always the same: an *a* is always an *a*. So when I'm drawing, the creative part of my brain is imagining what things look like. When I'm writing, it's trying to remember what the letters look like. There's no creative part to it."

Nonverbal Learning Disability

Eight-year-old Sam didn't like to play softball, but he willingly went out to right field when Marcy Wyzlinski asked him to do so. Sam tried very hard to pay attention to the game, so when his classmate Adam hit the ball toward him, he was right there to catch it.

Here it was. Almost here. Oh, no—thud. The ball fell at Sam's feet. "Throw the ball, throw the ball," the other kids screamed, and Sam finally threw it toward first base when he should have thrown it to second.

"Great throw," Adam said to him on the way back into the classroom. "Maybe you should sign up for our softball league." He was smiling.

Sam looked up surprised. "Really? Do you think I'm a good player? I don't think I'm a good player."

Adam kept smiling. "I think you're the best player in third grade."

Marcy had overheard their conversation and finally caught up to them. "Adam, please go into the library and wait for me there. I want to talk with you. Stay here for a minute with me, Sam."

Once Adam and the other kids had gone inside, Marcy said, "Adam was teasing you. He doesn't think you're a good player."

"But he was smiling," Sam said.

"Just because someone is smiling when they're talking to you, it doesn't mean they are telling the truth. You have to listen to their words and decide for yourself if what they are saying is true."

What is a nonverbal learning disability?

According to NLDline (www.nldline.com), an online advocacy group whose main goal is to provide education, a nonverbal learning disorder has patterns of characteristics, including both strengths and weaknesses. Students with nonverbal learning disabilities are very fluent and capable with language. They may have difficulty with motor skills, visual and spatial organization, the organization of time and tasks, sensory sensitivity, and social skills.

What are some unique characteristics of students with nonverbal learning disabilities?

Students with this disability begin to speak early and often appear to be precocious and even gifted as toddlers. As they grow, they pay close attention to details and can remember what they see and hear. Once in school, they read well and often are excellent spellers.

They may experience difficulty with large motor skills, such as balance, and difficulty with small motor skills, such as using scissors. Areas in which other kids relax, such as arts and crafts, can be challenging for them.

The organization of visual space can also be confusing. Pages that have lots of text that is not clearly laid out are difficult for them to read. Marie Oslinsky's fifth-grade student Hui-Ling was confused by a worksheet that Marie had created for students to record a science experiment. Marie had added fun graphics and some optional challenges. Most of her students found the page interesting and challenging. For Hui-Ling, however, Marie needed to create a simple sheet, with only the necessary headings, such as "Materials needed" and "These are the things we did."

In addition to the organization of visual space, organizing time and action may be challenging. This organizational ability, referred to as executive function, can affect the ability to establish goals and plan and execute the many steps needed to complete a long project. Students with nonverbal learning disabilities need help with multistep tasks such as complex book reports or social studies projects. They often need help with prioritizing and organizing homework. Any school task that involves future actions can be challenging.

A student with a nonverbal learning disability can have significant challenges relating to other people. Since so much communication is expressed nonverbally (more than 65%, some people say), she often misses or misinterprets important social cues such as facial expressions and tone of voice. She may not recognize other people's physical boundaries. You may see her standing too close to another child at recess, unaware that the other child is trying to get away from her. She may talk too loudly, talk too much, or try to answer all the questions in class just because she knows them. Her ability to recognize and accommodate other people's needs can be poor.

Students with these issues may have anxiety and/or obsessive-compulsive disorder, largely caused by their discomfort in the world. Peers and teachers may describe them as "annoying." They are often bullied and are frequently lonely and unhappy.

What does my student with a nonverbal learning disability need from me?

Curriculum

When you teach in a subject area, talk about the concepts. Explain the directions. Verbally describe as much as you can. The more you explicitly say, the more she will understand.

Sarah Moretti's fourth-grade student Martha has an IEP goal that states, "Martha will be able to verbally restate important concepts that she is learning." When Martha's paraprofessional is working directly with her, this is one of the goals she focuses on. Sarah can support this work by occasionally asking Martha to tell her, in her own words, what Sarah has just explained. The more people who support Martha's practice the better, because then Martha does not expect to have to pay close attention to only one adult, like her paraprofessional.

Students with nonverbal learning disabilities need papers that have limited visual distractions. Classroom assignments and homework assignments and tests should have the visual space clearly laid out. There should be a minimum of visual clutter and lots of white space.

When a task is presented, especially one involving many steps, help your student to figure out how to begin the task and how to organize it so she can continue working on it independently. If necessary, create a chart or other verbal-based system to help her focus on the steps she needs to accomplish to complete the task.

Know that your student will have trouble being on time. Give her extra time to get places, and give her specific verbal cues to find her way if she is in an unfamiliar place. Explicitly tell her how to act in any situation, such as on a field trip.

Expectations

Because students with this disability have problems with spatial organization and motor output, less written output should be expected of them. Requiring less output is usually more effective than giving them more time.

Social Relationships

Explain everything explicitly in social situations. This may seem odd because a student with nonverbal learning disabilities tends to talk too much. Yet helpful talk is frequently what she most needs from you. Talk about what has happened, what will happen, what is expected of her, how she should behave, why other people have acted as they have. Talk, talk, and talk. A student with a nonverbal learning disability will probably not figure it out for herself. The more you can clearly and simply describe what is happening, the safer she will feel.

For example, Gary Sullivan overheard his sixth-grade student Ellen bragging to a group of students about the score of 100% that she got on her spelling test. At lunch that day, he noticed her sitting alone at the end of a long table, with all the other kids settled in at the other end, far away from her.

Gary wanted to help. He took Ellen aside and talked with her about what he had seen. He told Ellen that he wanted to give her some information. He was matter-of-fact and stuck with observable facts. He said, "This morning, I saw you tell Ronnie, Alice, and Tom about your good spelling test. I saw you wave your paper in the air and say, 'Wow, I did great. I did great! I did so great, I'm going to ask for harder words next week.' I really understand that you were excited about your good spelling test. But spelling's really hard for some people, so when you talk too much about how well you did, it can make them feel bad." Gary gave Ellen some quiet time to think about what he had said. Then, he finished by explaining what she might have done. He said, "Next time, it might be better to put your spelling test in your desk without saying anything. You can feel good in your own heart that you did well. Do you know somebody you could tell later about doing such a good job?" Ellen decided to share her news with her brother in the future.

Students with nonverbal learning disabilities need many positive social interactions with lots of different people, so one thing you have to watch out for is having your student become too dependent on you. If you're more tolerant and understanding of her behavior than her peers are, she will naturally gravitate to you. She may need this support at times, but the ultimate goal is for her to be socially appropriate with a wide variety of people.

Students with these issues take things literally. If someone is smiling but saying something sarcastic, she will only "read" the smile. She has real difficulty with the subtleties of social interaction. This can create situations where other kids can take advantage of her.

Understanding Your Student

Advocate for your student. This is such a relatively unknown and misunderstood disability that even many professionals do not yet understand it. If you have a student who has some of the challenges described here, ask about the possibility of this disability being present.

Be protective of your student's feelings and assume she is doing the best she can. These kids are often thought of as demanding and lazy and bothersome to both kids and adults. In truth, they are often frightened and lonely kids who just don't know what to do.

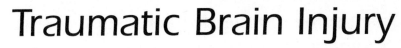

Traumatic Brain Injury

Jacob was a popular boy with a great sense of humor before the horrible day when he was hit by a car. When he returned to school four months later, he didn't smile or express any interest in the other kids. He wanted only to do worksheets by himself at his desk.

One day, Jacob wheeled his wheelchair to the back of the room where the book, The Broken Arrow Boy by Adam Moore, lay on a table. The cover of this book shows a smiling boy with a pretend arrow piercing his head.

Tony, a former friend, noticed Jacob's interest. "It's a good book," he said. "That kid, the one on the cover, he wrote it. Him and his friends."

"Why does he have that arrow in his head?" Jacob asked.

"He fell on it. He was in the hospital a long time."

"Just like me," Jacob said.

Tony nodded.

"He's just like me."

"What d'ya mean?" Tony asked.

"He did something stupid and he got hurt."

"He just fell. And you didn't do anything stupid. You got hit by a drunk driver."

"It was my fault. I should've been looking."

"It was an accident. An accident can happen to anybody."

Later that morning, when Jacob's mom came to take him home for the day, she noticed that Jacob waved good-bye to Tony. Then, he turned and waved good-bye to some of the other kids.

What is traumatic brain injury?

Traumatic brain injury (TBI) is a head injury that is caused either by a severe blow or by suddenly stopping after moving quickly. These injuries can be mild, moderate, or severe. The effects range from a short loss of consciousness to serious impairment in all areas of intellectual, physical, and social functioning. Athletic accidents, car accidents, and blows to the head are the most common causes of TBI (D'Amato, Rik, et al., 1998).

What are some unique characteristics of students with traumatic brain injury?

Every brain injury is different. The areas of the injury determine the problems. Students with TBI may exhibit many of the symptoms of a learning disability. (See pages 14–32 for more on learning disabilities.)

One way that a TBI is different from a traditional learning disability is that the student has suffered a sudden loss or change of abilities. This can lead to disappointment, grief, and anger for both the student and his family.

This type of injury may also make students very sensitive to stimulation. Thus, a happy, busy, and noisy classroom with lots of activity areas can be tiring.

Recovery is much more difficult than it's often portrayed in the movies or on television. With a severe injury, a person may have to move through all the developmental stages again, including those of an infant. For most people, verbal skills and well-known material come back first; the ability to learn new things and the ability to reason come back more slowly.

The trajectory of recovery from TBI can be uneven. Symptoms and issues can appear weeks, months, or even years later,

> ### TBI Rehab
>
> Because of improved medical procedures, kids with TBI are moved out of medical rehab facilities faster than in the past. Schools are now expected to handle the post-medical issues of these children much earlier.

depending on the place and severity of the injury. Problem areas extant at the time the IEP is written might improve—or get worse—in a very short time. Because a person's brain continues to develop until the age of 20, the extent of the injury sometimes does not become evident right away. It can appear when the part of the person's brain that has been previously inactive begins to mature. If this part of the brain has been injured, problems may show up.

What does my student with traumatic brain injury need from me?

Understanding Your Student

Keep in mind that a brain injury is not like other injuries. Read all available reports about your student, including the occupational therapist's report, to find out how your student's academic, physical, and social skills have been affected. Really know what your student is dealing with and use this knowledge as a guidepost as you teach and interact with him. Remember that his needs may change abruptly.

Your student desperately wants to return to normal as quickly as possible. Natalie Weber's third-grade student Andy was injured in a serious sledding accident in January. When he got back to school after three weeks in a regular hospital and one month in a rehabilitation hospital, he told Natalie, "I got hurt, but now I'm fine." In reality, Andy was not fine. He desperately wanted everything to be the same, but he was also painfully aware that he couldn't do things as quickly or as well as he did before. Andy needed Natalie to be calm and consistent and to treat him as a normal boy. He had new academic, social, and emotional needs because of his injuries, but he also needed to be able to relax in the safe familiarity of the classroom.

During TBI recovery, kids may remain unaware of their disabilities and not realize things are different from before. They may not understand why people and other students are reacting differently to them.

Setting Up the Classroom

Place your student in as quiet a place in your classroom as you can, and be very aware of how much external stimulation he is receiving. As much as possible, minimize this stimulation.

Structuring the Day

Don't expect as much from the student in the afternoon. Fatigue is a big factor in recovery from injury. If it has been a particularly hectic morning, he may need to sit in a quiet corner and read silently instead of participating in math class. He will get back to math class once he is less fatigued.

Curriculum

Keep a sharp eye out for changes in your student's performance. Since you see your student so much during the school day and in so many different settings, you are in a powerful position to make important observations. His recovery can be uneven and new issues may quickly appear. Therefore, his academic program needs to be very flexible. Report any changes to the special education team. The IEP may need to be changed frequently.

In Andy's case, he was an avid reader and excellent speller before his accident. When he returned to school, his spelling skills were seriously impaired, but his reading skills appeared to be only somewhat delayed. One day, however, Natalie noticed Andy sitting at his desk holding a book in a funny way, his head bent way down. When she went to investigate, she realized that he was crying. Natalie asked him to come to a more private spot and then asked him what was wrong.

"I don't know that word," he said, pointing to *the*. "I always used to know that word."

When Natalie investigated further, she realized that, in fact, Andy's reading skills had further deteriorated. He now needed a much more structured program with less challenging books. Andy's IEP needed to be changed.

Two years later, after Andy had received very good instruction, he once again was an enthusiastic reader. His spelling skills never fully recovered, but he was able to become an adequate speller and to compensate with a spell check on the computer. He also became a dictionary aficionado, developing a fascination for the etymology of words.

Relating to Parents

Remember that TBI is a trauma for the whole family, including the brothers and sisters of the student who has been injured. It's helpful for everyone to know that if a problem arises it can be dealt with immediately. A communication book between home and school can be extremely helpful. This can be a small bound notebook that your student carries back and forth. You and the parents can note changes and especially new challenges that may come up. Also remember to celebrate successes. Parents will appreciate knowing that their son raised his hand and contributed to a class discussion, for example.

Expectations

Create clear and simple rules for behavior expectations for your student, and be consistent in enforcing these rules. Consequences should be immediate and calming, such as time-out in a quiet area. Your student may feel frustrated, confused, and angry because of the loss of some of his abilities, and he may feel like lashing out at his peers. You need to make it clear that this is not an appropriate way to handle these feelings. If behavioral issues continue, report them to the special education team. Your student may need different or more emotional support.

Social Relationships

If parents or other knowledgeable people ask to speak with your class about the particular accident the student suffered, and/or about TBI in general, it may be helpful. In one case, a fifth grader named Maya had fallen off her bike. Unfortunately, she hadn't been wearing her helmet and suffered a serious blow to her head. When Maya was in the hospital, rumors abounded on the playground about various gory details of the accident. Maya's mother came to school and calmly and nondramatically told the class what really happened. She answered questions and told the kids about some ways Maya might be different now. She was, for example, having trouble using her hands. She couldn't yet hold a pencil, and she could only pay attention for a few minutes when someone was talking with her. Because of her mother's intervention, Maya returned to a much calmer classroom.

A Quote From a Father of a Child with TBI

This is a quote from the father of a seventh grader named Matthew who suffered a traumatic brain injury from a fall while climbing rocks.

"It's one thing if it happens to you at twenty or so, and, like a stroke, you have to adjust your emotional and physical life to the new you. But if you're a kid who is still trying to figure out who he is—and now the brain injury shifts things around . . . it's not like a broken arm that just gets better and it's over. In many ways, you're never the same. Like the other night, Matthew had such a hard time with homework and I said, 'Look, it's late. You're tired. Your brain gets tired.' And he said, 'What if I have to pull an allnighter in college?' I told him, "I went to college and I never had to pull an all nighter." And he said, "But what if I have to?"

ADD and ADHD

When Kimi had to change schools in November because her family had moved, she came prepared to tell her new fifth-grade teacher what she needed.

"I have ADD," she said. "That means I stare out the window a lot, even when I'm supposed to be paying attention. My old teacher would walk near me and stand in front of me for a minute. This would remind me to pay attention again."

"Let's try that, too," said her teacher.

"And before I go home, would you check that I have everything I need for homework, like all the books?" Kimi laughed. "Once, when I was just a little kid, we went to see my Grandma for the weekend, and I told my mom I was old enough to pack for myself." She laughed again. "We got there, and my mom unpacked my suitcase, and guess what she found?"

"I don't know. What?"

"Fourteen pairs of underwear! Mom always told me to bring underwear, but I kind of forgot the other stuff," she chuckled. "Now, I have a list of stuff to bring."

"Well, I know one thing you didn't forget to bring to school today," said her teacher.

"What?"

"Your great sense of humor."

What are Attention Deficit Disorder (ADD) and Attention Deficit Hyperactivity Disorder (ADHD)?

ADD and ADHD are both disorders of attention. People affected by them have difficulty attending to stimuli outside of themselves. A person with ADD appears inattentive to the outside world. With ADHD, impulsive and hyperactive behavior is added to the mix.

Both ADD and ADHD are medical diagnoses that only a doctor can make. Lots of kids may be inattentive and very active, but it is up to a doctor to determine if this behavior is caused by a physical condition. The exact cause or causes of ADD and ADHD are unknown, but researchers are studying the roles of genetics, neuroanatomical factors, neuropsychological factors, and neurochemical factors (Flick, 2002).

What are some unique characteristics of students with ADD/ADHD?

ADD and ADHD are considered together because both involve difficulty with attention to the outside world—especially to things that are of little interest, such as spelling lessons. People with these disorders have exceptional ability to attend to things they enjoy. They may spend hours at the computer but have difficulty transitioning to something that they care about much less.

Even though ADD looks very different on the outside from ADHD, some people with ADD report that they also experience restlessness. They do things such as hum or press their fingers together to provide an outlet for this energy. These are kids who can manage to stay in their seats and not slide under the desk during instruction, but they also tend to daydream a lot.

Students with ADHD often talk a lot and exhibit many motor movements. They make noises, rock back and forth in their chairs, bang things, and bump people. They act and react quickly. It's important to provide them with a calm and consistent environment where rules and expectations are predictable.

Like kids who have dyslexia and nonverbal learning disabilities, students with ADD and ADHD have difficulty with the organization of space, time, and tasks. Their desks are often very messy, and keeping track of things can be downright impossible. Curt Slovak's sixth-grade student Alicia can do all of her homework on a Wednesday afternoon, but then lose it by Thursday morning when she's supposed to turn it in. Alicia's mom says this is particularly surprising, since she watched Alicia put the homework in her school backpack.

Students with ADD and ADHD may have difficulty organizing time. They often need help with prioritizing their homework: what to do first, next, and last. They need help figuring out how long it will take them to do their homework and planning when they should do it. If you have assigned a long project with many steps, such as a social studies or science report, students with ADD and ADHD will need help planning and completing the project. Often a time line that records when things need to be done can be very helpful.

A positive aspect of having ADHD is that these students have a lot of energy. If their energy can be directed appropriately, they can be extremely productive.

What does my student with ADD/ADHD need from me?

Organization and Structure

Be aware of where you place your student in the classroom. Your student with ADD needs to be in a place where there is the least amount of extraneous stimulation. Having her sit near the art table with all those crayons and art supplies is probably not a good choice. Place her where she is least likely to disturb her peers with her extra movements. The edges of the seating arrangement are probably best. Seating her in the middle of the group is probably the worst choice.

Playing soft music, especially classical music, can be very calming for these students. It is best to play this music for the whole class, but if that is not possible, give your student a headset.

Working so hard to pay attention is very tiring, so your student with ADD or ADHD may need periods of rest. Retreating to a quiet corner to read or draw can be restorative. Your student with ADHD can become more active when she gets tired. With fatigue, the yo-yo string gets strung tighter and moves faster. Watch your student to see how often, and when, she needs short breaks from the group.

Remember that verbal directions can be part of the external stimuli that a student with ADD or ADHD has trouble focusing on. Your voice, after all, can be much less interesting to her than the mobile she is making. She is not ignoring you; she isn't hearing you. In this case, a visual prompt, discussed or decided upon ahead of time, can help. One such prompt might be standing directly in front of her and touching your lips. This means, "Look at my lips and listen to what I am saying." Then, keep your directions short and to the point. At times, provide support by your physical presence. Quietly sitting next to your student can calm her and help her to focus.

> **A Quick Tip**
>
> Remind parents to provide healthy snacks that are low in refined sugar. A banana or cheese and crackers is preferable to candy and cookies. Celery or an apple are good choices because they provide crunch.

Dealing With Inattention and Hyperactivity

Distinguish between hyperactive behavior and oppositional behavior. (See page 106 for information on oppositional disorder.) It's hard for a kid with ADHD to sit still at morning meeting, to be quiet and stay focused at her desk, to not play with the food trays in the lunchroom. She wants to poke and punch as a game, to play fight like a puppy. This behavior needs to be controlled, whatever the cause, but it is important to find the cause. If the behavior is the result of hyperactivity, your student will usually respond quickly and cooperatively to clear rules and expectations. Students with oppositional disorder, however, usually have arguments for everything. They often don't respond to your logic and will try to transform the situation by substituting logic of their own. A basic guideline: Students with ADHD usually want to please you, whereas students with active oppositional disorder do not. They want to be right. They want to be in control.

If you remain confused about whether your student's behavior is hyperactive or oppositional, check with the special education team for advice. A special education teacher may want to observe your student in class. If the behavior turns out to be oppositional, speak with the special education team so that your student can get the specialized help she needs.

Provide legitimate outlets for hyperactive behavior. Your student is working very hard to stay in her seat and to listen to your instructions. Let her doodle, as long as it doesn't bother others. Let her take the book you borrowed for a read-aloud back to the school library. Ask her to wipe off the chalkboard. Give her opportunities to move.

Watch for anything your student does right and praise her for it. Catch her doing something she is good at. All too often, especially if she has ADHD, she faces disapproval from adults. An effective reward for positive behavior can be uninterrupted listening time from you. She may talk so much that people develop the habit of not listening to her. A few minutes of uninterrupted listening time can be powerful.

Every student with ADD or ADHD is unique. Careful observation to find out what each child needs is important. Asking a student what she needs is also helpful. She may have some great ideas about how to be more successful in your classroom.

> ### A Quick Tip
>
> It helps some kids with ADHD to have a small rubber ball in their desk that they can squeeze to utilize excess energy. This doesn't help all kids—some of them start throwing or bouncing the ball.

Curriculum

The optimal curriculum includes a balance of teacher-directed and self-directed activities. Your student needs to develop an ability to do things that are uninteresting to her. If this is tempered in the classroom by periods in which she is allowed to choose an activity that interests her, she'll learn better and develop her ability to attend.

Read your student's IEP so that you can be aware of any specific areas where she needs extra support. Lisa MacIntyre's third-grade student Andrea has an IEP goal that states, "Andrea will develop the ability to follow three-step verbal directions." From that, Lisa knows that she needs to be aware of Andrea when she gives this type of direction. It might be best for Andrea if Lisa waits for her to complete each step before giving the next direction.

Special Things You Need to Teach Your Student With ADD or ADHD

Rosalina Chapman's fourth-grade student Maria needed help organizing her physical environment. It didn't help, however, for Rosalina to simply tell Maria to clean up her desk and make sure she kept track of her pencils. Instead, Rosalina sat with her and said, "First we're going to look in your desk and see what you don't need. Do you need this paper? Okay, let's throw that one out. Do you need this notebook? Okay, let's put it in the right-hand side of your desk where you can get it easily." Rosalina modeled a system and did it often. To help Maria manage her supplies, Rosalina provided physical props. She gave her a box to put her pencils in. In time, Maria got better at keeping her desk organized.

Maria also needed help organizing her time. Here again, physical props helped. Rosalina and Maria together wrote down the goals for Maria's book report project. They created a chart where the tasks that needed to be accomplished were written out.

For young children, these charts can have pictures. One mother of a boy with ADHD reports that when her son Sam entered kindergarten, she created a poster for him to help him get ready independently for school. A picture of soap reminded him to wash his face and hands; a picture of a toothbrush reminded him to brush his teeth. There were pictures of underwear, a shirt, pants, shoes, and socks. Sam put a check next to each item as he accomplished the job. (A pencil was attached by a string to the chart).

In order to be somewhere on time, your student may need a chart that specifies what she needs to do and estimates of the time it will take to finally reach her destination. For example:

<u>Goal: Get to the school bus on time.</u>

✓ get my backpack from the cubby: 2 minutes
✓ put on my coat and hat: 1 minute
✓ walk down the hall and down the three flights of stairs: 5 minutes

Then, the departure time can be determined. This is excellent training and preparation for helping her be on time not only for school, but also for jobs and social appointments.

Teach her how to pay attention in class. One way of doing this is to create a poster with the class for the whole class that describes how a student looks when paying attention. You can include things like:

I am sitting in my seat.

My hands are not moving.

My eyes are on the speaker.

Transitions

Since students with attention issues often have great difficulty leaving an activity that interests them, it helps to give them advance notice before ending an activity. Here again, verbal cues are not usually effective. Instead, give tangible cues, which you have discussed ahead of time. For example, if Olivia is working on math facts at the computer (which she loves), place a green (for "go") token or sticky note at the bottom of the computer monitor when she is to continue working. Five minutes before Olivia needs to leave the computer, place a yellow (for "caution") token or sticky note on it. When it's time to turn off the computer and leave, place a red (for "stop") token or sticky note on it.

Teach your student to notice key cues in the environment. For example, if the other kids are putting things away in their desks, that means something new is happening. This can prepare her for transitions.

Homework and Tests

Quickly check at the end of the day that your student is bringing home all the things she needs to do her homework. A home–school partnership can be very helpful. Talk with parents about establishing a consistent routine (taking fatigue factors into consideration) and a calm environment. Again, playing classical music can be helpful.

During test taking, your student will do her best if the test is announced ahead of time. Pop quizzes may be too challenging. A quiet, familiar environment helps. Also, if the test is long, it's good to give short breaks.

Helping Your Student Understand Herself

It is important to help every student come to understand herself as a learner: how she learns best (auditory, visual, or tactile-kinesthetic), what she needs to do to be able to focus outside of herself, and how she can maintain focus. It is particularly important for your student with ADD or ADHD, however, because she needs to grow in her ability to function independently in the mainstream. As you talk with her and work with her, realize that one of the most important things you can teach her is how to become more independent.

Medication for ADD/ADHD

Some students with ADD/ADHD take medication. Some people believe that not giving medication to a child who is diagnosed with ADD/ADHD is like not giving insulin to a diabetic. They say that the medication is needed to normalize the chemicals in the brain. Other people say that medication is greatly overused and that behavioral and environmental interventions, such as a highly structured, well-organized, and low-stress academic setting, are effective ways to control inattentiveness and hyperactivity. Ultimately, parents need to decide what they feel is best for their child.

A Short Interview With a Mother Who Has ADHD and Who Has a Son With ADD

When did you first discover that you had issues with attention?
"I discovered the ADD first when our son was diagnosed with it. We did have a sense that he was a child with special needs early on: when he was two he had many verbal tantrums. As the doctor explained my son's behaviors, I thought, that's how I am. But I always thought everybody was like this. I feel like a car with the accelerator pedal stuck on full throttle. We've got the overstimulation blues, but oddly enough, stimulation of the right kinds helps me rest. I hum. When I'm home I put music on and that gives me a break."

What is the most important thing for teachers to know about kids with ADD/ADHD?
"Unless there is a recognized behavior problem, these kids mean well. They're doing the best they can. They're living with a real disability—it's not visible, not like a physical disability, but it's real. They really need your help. They want to do well."

What is the most important thing for teachers to do to help kids with ADD/ADHD?
"Help all the kids in the class know that we each have a learning style and we all need different things. Some kids need glasses and some kids need to ask a lot of questions, and some kids need help learning how to pay attention in class. Help the kids see that the kid with ADD or ADHD is just like every other kid who needs certain things. That's all."

ADD/ADHD

Autism

Every morning, Tom hung his coat on the peg rack outside the classroom, walked over to the radiator at the end of the hall and sang a TV commercial. Then, he came into the classroom.

Tom understood what people said to him, but it took him a lot of time to respond. His teacher, Dennis Silverstein noticed that he paused and almost grimaced as he tried to form his words. The normal rhythm of conversation was missing. Some of the kids were patient, but others were not. Kids tended to tease Tom on the playground, especially because of the way he entered school each day.

During quiet times in the classroom, Tom sometimes sat at his desk with his whole body bent over. It looked like he was scribbling. Since he usually did what he was asked to do, Dennis felt that Tom was probably resting at this time, and that he should allow him to do so. One day, however, another student, Sean, walked by and accidentally hit Tom's elbow. A piece of paper fell on the floor.

Sean picked it up. "Oh," he said, "did you do this?"

Tom grabbed for it, but Sean held it up high. "No, it's great," he said. He showed the class the full-perspective drawing of a nearby abandoned factory.

"Tom, did you draw this?" Dennis asked.

He nodded. He reached in his desk and pulled out a stack of papers, each showing an amazing drawing of a neighborhood building.

Tom became the class architect. Now all of the kids were more patient waiting for his answers. And when he sang near the radiators, they often went and stood next to him.

What is autism?

There are five disorders that are called Pervasive Developmental Disorders (PDD) by the American Psychiatric Association. These are Autistic Disorder, Asperger's Disorder (or Syndrome), Childhood Disintegration Disorder (CDD), Rett's Disorder, and PDD—Not Otherwise Specified (PDD-NOS). Autism has attracted much public and media attention.

According to the Autism Society of America (www.autism-society.org), autism is a neurological disorder that affects communication and the processing of sensory information. The senses may be oversensitive or undersensitive and, in addition, have difficulty working together. The social behavior of people with autism can be unusual, causing others to perceive them as lacking empathy. They appear to live in their own worlds. They are not devoid of emotion, however, and have feelings just like everyone else.

What are some unique characteristics of students with autism?

People with autism are all unique individuals. There is a wide spectrum of behaviors and great variation in the severity of symptoms. Some people experience very mild symptoms and live normal lives with a minimum of support. Others experience severe symptoms and need ongoing treatment and intervention. With proper treatment and education, however, all students can make progress and learn.

The current belief is that many people with autism also have mental retardation. However, since it is extremely difficult, if not impossible to evaluate some students, perhaps these people should be considered untestable as opposed to mentally retarded by default.

People with autism may also be untestable for sight and hearing, so they may have undiagnosed vision or hearing impairments.

Some people with autism speak very well, while others never learn to speak at all. Their communication styles can be highly unusual. Some people repeat what a person has just said to them (echolalia), instead of responding to the communication. Others repeat phrases from books or movies. Still others speak in seemingly nonsense syllables, as when Ira, a fourth grader, ran to his mom saying, "*Mabkib, mabkib.*" His mother said, "Ira, I don't understand." Ira repeated, "*Mabkib.*" Finally, Ira ran to the table and grabbed a napkin from the table.

Myth

In the past, some people believed that autism was caused by a mother's rejection of her child. This is in no way true. Now, it's understood that autism is a neurological condition.

Then, his mom understood. Ira had eaten some jam that had made his hands sticky. He needed a napkin. "*Mabkib*" meant "napkin." Ira had the vowels right, but had difficulty with the consonants.

The communication problems of people with autism can be similar to those of children who have had brain tumors removed: they often understand language but cannot respond. It's like the words are stuck in their minds. Sometimes, there is a time lag: they can eventually speak, but they have difficulty fitting into the normal ebb and flow of conversation.

When thinking about autism, it is also important to consider the concept of sensory integration. We all use our senses of sight, hearing, smell, taste, and touch to experience the world. For typical people, our senses work together, relating easily to one another. For example, consider noticing (seeing) a piece of cheese on a cheese and cracker board. Because you like cheese, you reach for it and pick it up (touch). As you bring it to your mouth, you are aware of a lovely aroma (smell). Finally, you put it in your mouth and enjoy it (taste).

People with autism can have difficulty integrating their senses. Sometimes, one or more of their senses is oversensitive. For example, Michael Thomas's fifth-grade student Clara is so sensitive to sound, that even sounds that are considered normal background noise, such as the clicking of the keys on a keyboard, are highly distressing to her. Clara needs to sit away from the class computers, in as quiet a spot as possible. Even though Michael did move her to a protected spot, she can still be highly troubled by unusual sounds. Michael was surprised one day to see her curled up in a ball on the floor by her desk, covering her ears. When he went to investigate, he discovered that the classroom window was open and that the custodian was mowing the lawn right below. After he shut the window and the mower moved away, he was able to coax Clara back to her desk. On this occasion, she was able to tell him that the sound actually hurt.

Another sense that can be oversensitive for people with autism is the sense of touch. Their nerve endings may be on high alert, and being touched can feel overstimulating and uncomfortable. This is called *tactual defensiveness*. People believe that this is the reason that some babies with

Myth

Not all people with autism have an aversion to being touched. Some do enjoy physical contact and enjoy being affectionate.

autism don't like to be cuddled and push away someone who is trying to hold them. Unfortunately, they then don't get the loving physical contact that all human beings need, and this can cause further developmental and emotional issues. Oversensitivity to taste can create strong aversions to and strong preferences for certain foods. An oversensitivity to smell can create strong desires to smell things, even people.

People with autism may also have senses that are undersensitive. When these are on the same team with other senses that happen to be oversensitive, this can cause real confusion. These challenges with sensory integration are considered to be critically important to the understanding of autism.

Students with autism are often hyperactive, which affects their ability to learn in a classroom environment. (This can moderate in adolescence.) They often are visual thinkers. Temple Grandin, Ph.D., an assistant professor at Colorado State University, is internationally known for designing livestock equipment. She also has autism. In her article *Teaching Tips for Children and Adults with Autism*, which can be found on www.autism.org/temple/tips.html, she says, "I think in pictures. I do not think in language. All my thoughts are like videotapes running in my imagination. Pictures are my first language, and words are my second language. Nouns were the easiest words to learn because I could make a picture in my mind of the word." Even though many or even most people with autism are visual thinkers, however, they seem to be visually unaware of faces, facial expressions, and body language.

People with autism can become fascinated by one topic, such as numbers, trucks, or a particular machine like a washing machine. This is called a *fixation* and needs to be distinguished from repetitive actions, such as spinning or hand-flapping. The focused attention outside of themselves can be good; the latter can be destructive.

Behavior Affecting Social Relationships

Here are some typical behaviors that are considered "autistic tendencies" that make social relationships very difficult:

* apparent lack of interest in others
* apparent lack of awareness of others, and especially how one is supposed to interact
* lack of eye contact
* unusual attachment to physical objects
* odd and repetitive play
* self-destructive behavior
* the desire for things to always be the same

It is easy to understand why people with autism have emotional issues. If you are living with senses that, at any point, can greatly distress you, and if you are never sure that you will be able to communicate your feelings, needs, or wants, it would be extremely difficult to relax. It's no wonder that people with autism sometimes exhibit aggressive behavior.

Some people believe that people with autism don't know what is expected of them, that they simply don't know what to do in certain situations. For example, four-year-old Joey was playing in a sandbox in his backyard. His mom was nearby, doing some gardening. All of a sudden, his mom fell and hurt her back very badly. She couldn't get up, and she cried out in pain. Joey kept playing in the sandbox, even though his dad was in the house. After a few minutes, Joey's dad heard screams and came out to investigate. People hear a story like this and assume Joey lacks empathy. Another way of looking at it, however, is to realize that Joey was upset and didn't know what to do. He didn't know that the appropriate thing was to go get help. Because he was distressed, he focused even harder on his play in the sandbox as a way to comfort himself.

What does my student with autism need from me?

Understanding Your Student . . . and Yourself

First and foremost, he needs understanding and compassion. The behavior of your student can sometimes be so odd that it is difficult to have patience with him. The important thing to remember is that his experience of whatever is occurring may be different from yours. The sensory information he is getting and his difficulty with communication may be causing his social anomalies. Get as much information as you can about his particular sensory input. Does he, for example, have an oversensitive sense of smell? This could explain why he got so upset when the science activity table that had been recently painted was brought back into the room. You and most of the other kids noticed a slight odor; your student with autism ran away from the table.

If you know that your student has one or more overactive senses, be aware of any environmental stimuli that could potentially distress him. For example, if your student has oversensitive hearing, it's really important to find out when fire drills are going to occur, and to plan how to handle them. You don't want him curling into a tight ball wherever he is and staying there, unable to be consoled or moved.

Sometimes, you can't stop the sudden, unexpected stimuli. You can't, for example, stop the man using the jackhammer on the sidewalk as your class rides by on the bus on a field trip. Don't panic, and don't blame yourself if there are occasional unexpected incidents. Just be as aware and as alert as you can be to these situations and have a plan for how to help your student with his distress.

It is important to remember that *you*, also, need understanding. In order to maintain firm, consistent, kind, and creative interactions with your student, you will need support. If you are feeling confused about how to handle a particular situation, talk with someone on your special education team and ask for help.

Expectations

You need to be firm with your student. Expectations need to be clear and consistent, with only the essential ones being presented. You should know and be able to clearly articulate your expectations about your student's behavior toward himself and others, and about his academic functioning. Your student and others in the classroom need to know that expectations and rules stay the same whether it is Wednesday morning or Friday afternoon.

Curriculum

Since students with autism tend to be visual learners, visual cues greatly help them understand language, concepts, directions, and schedules. Keep auditory explanations to a minimum, and have visual cues everywhere. When you are talking about the weather, for example, have pictures that represent the different types of clouds or the different kinds of rain. Have a picture for a gentle rainstorm and one for a downpour. Have a chart that represents the schedule of the class day. A picture of a book can represent reading time. A group of numbers can represent math. A picture of a group of kids listening to a teacher can represent read-aloud time.

Teach concepts in many different settings. This way, the concept does not become associated with only the setting in which it is being taught. In other words, 4 + 4 equals 8 at your student's desk, on the floor, in the back of the room, and even outside in the hallway. Also, have different people involved in direct instruction so that the student will generalize the skill with different instructors. Peers can help here.

For every curriculum unit, ask yourself, "What is a good goal for my student for this unit?" and, "How can I tell if he has met that goal?" Angela

Perlman's sixth-grade student Wally has a communication style that is very halted. On a good day, he can speak, but he does so in a monotone. He is mastering writing on the computer and is currently at about a second-grade level with his writing skills. His class is studying China, and Angela wonders how Wally can profit from this unit. First, she checks the curriculum framework to see what all kids need to learn. Next, she looks at Wally's IEP and sees what's there. She discovers that one of Wally's objectives (for his writing goal) is that he will be able to write complete sentences with at least one subject and one verb. The China unit is perfect for this. Angela can expect Wally to write a sentence about China every day at the computer, and whether or not he is successful is easily measured. Another one of Wally's objectives (under his self-care goal) is that he will be introduced to different kinds of foods. When the class is doing projects, Angela makes sure that Wally is part of the group that is making and sampling a Chinese dish.

If your student has a fixation, such as a highly focused interest in polar bears, don't fight the fixation; use it for instruction. "But he should be interested in other things," is a common objection. This is a legitimate wish, but you can waste a lot of time trying to get your student to focus away from his fixation. Have him read about polar bears. Let him do polar bear number problems. On a map, show him where polar bears live. Discuss what they eat. Your best bet to widen your student's area of interest is to introduce other related topics, such as icebergs, that may engage your student.

Transitions

Kids with autism like things to be the same. Therefore, prepare your student for transitions ("There's five minutes until lunch.") and for changes in the schedule ("After lunch, we're going to the auditorium to hear a concert."). Since life in a busy classroom can change quickly, do the best you can with this. Visual schedules and cues help students learn to anticipate transitions more independently.

Social Relationships With Peers

Let the other kids help. If the parents approve, ask either a parent or an expert on autism to come to speak with your class. The other kids can be a tremendous help to your student. They will need guidance about how to interact, but they can offer friendship, attention, and lots of positive interactions, both socially and academically.

A Short Interview With a Mother of a Boy Who Has Autism

What are some important things a teacher should know when working with kids with autism?

"Kids with autism are hard to test. People assume that because they score poorly on IQ tests, they are not smart. They can be very bright. Our son couldn't speak, but our school team and family taught him to write, with typing first. Elijah can't speak, but he can write. He writes poetry, comments, and requests. This week, he wrote an essay on fall, using a word bank. He wrote five sentences on his own. His teacher was thrilled that he could do the assignment she'd given to all the students.

Never assume that because a kid can't speak, he can't read or write, that because he can't hold a pencil, he can't compose a poem. The approach should always be, How could he do it—rather than to assume he can't because he can't do this other thing.

The teacher should feel confident. You're going to make mistakes; everyone does. It's okay. Learn from them. You're going to feel that you have to do everything for the kid—that's a lot of emotional pressure, too. The most important thing to remember is that these are kids. Just do the best you can.

What's the most important thing for a teacher to do for a child with autism?

"Don't focus on what he can't do. Kids with autism *can* access the general curriculum. Every day, ask yourself things like, 'What valued role can Elijah have in history today?'

Now with our son, with Elijah, he can't speak, so if it's a vocabulary lesson, how can he contribute? Well, his teacher talked with the other kids and they came up with the idea of Elijah taking the index cards with the vocabulary words written on them up to the word board. He could also get vocabulary words from a book he is reading and add those words to the list."

Asperger's Syndrome

Even though she lives in Pennsylvania, Sonia seems to know everything there is to know about the state of Hawaii. She knows about the geography, the climate, the native peoples, the major cities. And Sonia will tell anyone and everyone all about these important things.

Every spring, the fourth grade makes a class quilt, with every student choosing a favorite book and decorating a quilt block that tells about it. Annmarie Ling-Finley was concerned about Sonia, because Sonia didn't like to draw and resisted doing any art. Annmarie was surprised and pleased, therefore, by Sonia's reaction to the quilt project.

Sonia said, "Hawaiian people make quilts."

"I didn't know that," Annmarie said.

"It's a special kind that has big geometric shapes that are one color. There's a picture of one in my book. Here, look. The only cloth Hawaiian women could make was tapa, from the tapa tree."

"That is an absolutely beautiful quilt, Sonia."

Pam, a classmate, walked by. "That's pretty," she said.

"But how can I make a pattern?" Sonia asked.

"You could use the one in your book for inspiration," Annmarie said.

"I'll help," Pam said. "My mom makes quilts, and she's teaching me."

Sonia looked away.

"Do you want Pam to help you?" Annmarie asked.

Sonia nodded.

"Then you need to thank her for her offer and accept her help."

"Thank you, Pam," Sonia said.

What is Asperger's Syndrome?

Asperger's Syndrome (also called Asperger Syndrome or Asperger's Disorder) is a neurologically based disorder that primarily affects a person's ability to be successful with social relationships. Many people feel that people with Asperger's want to connect socially but don't know how. The disorder also affects cognitive, sensory, and communication skills. First described by a Viennese doctor, Hans Asperger, in 1944, it is still little known and often misunderstood. Some people feel that it is a highly functional form of autism. Others say it is a type of nonverbal learning disability. Still others claim that it is a unique disorder. It is defined by the American Psychiatric Association (APA) as one of the five Pervasive Developmental Disorders (PDD), along with Autistic Disorder, Childhood Disintegration Disorder, Rett's Disorder and PDD—Not Otherwise Specified (PDD-NOS). Specific diagnostic criteria for Asperger's are outlined in the APA's Diagnostic and Statistical Manual of Mental Disorders (DSM-IV-TR). This description of Asperger's Syndrome is adapted from information on the Web site Online Asperger Syndrome Information and Support (O.A.S.I.S.) **www.udel.edu/bkirby/asperger/aswhatisit.html**.

What are some unique characteristics of students with Asperger's Syndrome?

Students have at least average intelligence, and many of them have a special talent or skill. The level of severity varies from mild to severe, and characteristics differ among individuals.

Students with Asperger's Syndrome have difficulty with social interactions. They have difficulty reading body language and are not always aware of physical boundaries. They may stand too close to others and not understand why others find this upsetting.

Kids with Asperger's are often described as "little professors." They often become focused on a particular interest, such as birds or geology, learning numerous facts about their subject. They will recite these facts to other people at great length. They talk and talk but have little interest in what other people have to say. They monologue rather than have dialogues.

Students with Asperger's are often teased and bullied because they don't understand social rules. They'll talk to other kids about things they're not interested in and try to tell them what to do. They'll interrupt conversations. They act in a way that makes people feel that they have little or no empathy. This behavior unfortunately sets them up for angry and aggressive behavior from their peers.

Students with Asperger's may be anxious and depressed. Just as they have trouble relating to other people's feelings, they may have trouble accepting and understanding their own. Plus, it's unpleasant to be teased and bullied.

Kids with Asperger's may have cognitive issues that affect their ability to solve problems, to think abstractly, and to understand spoken and written language. They may have trouble concentrating on a task they are not interested in. Teachers and parents are sometimes fooled about their reading comprehension levels because even though they decode easily and well, they don't always understand what they've just read.

They usually have excellent vocabularies and understand a wide variety of words in isolation but may speak with unusual tone, rhythm, and pitch. They may have particular difficulty understanding clichés and other social uses of language. They often take things literally. For example, when David, a sixth grader, overheard his principal say he had visited a company to "sell" the school so the company might donate a computer, David thought that the principal was actually "selling" the school for his own profit.

Their physical senses may be oversensitive to stimuli. It's important to know this, because it may explain what would otherwise seem like odd behaviors. Students with Asperger's may, for example, be troubled by repetitive sounds that no one else can hear (water dripping in a sink in the back of the room). They may dislike wearing certain pieces of clothing (maybe the cuff on the sleeve is too tight. And that tag!). They may have extreme preferences for some foods and extreme dislikes of others.

Students with Asperger's like everything to be the same and have great difficulty with transitions. In more extreme cases, they may have ritualistic ways of doing things, like washing their hands or playing. For example, Tommy, a boy in kindergarten, always lines up all the farm animals in a particular way: horse first, cow next, then three chickens, the pig, and the goat. All he does is line them up, put them back in their barn and then take them out and line them up again. He actively resists adding anything to his play or changing it in any way. If other kids try to play with him, he tells them to go away.

Students with Asperger's exhibit some symptoms of learning disabilities. They may have difficulty with organization, including both time and space. Many of them have trouble with motor coordination, affecting things like balance and handwriting.

What does my student with Asperger's Syndrome need from me?

Understanding Your Student

There is good news. Your student with Asperger's can learn social skills in the same way other people learn to ride a bicycle or play a musical instrument. These social skills need to be explicitly taught, and the earlier that teaching occurs, the better. It's best to focus on one particular social skill at a time.

Willard Ojala's third-grade student Harry usually walks away as soon as one of his peers approaches. He never looks at someone who is trying to talk to him. One day, when the rest of the students were reading silently, Willard asked Harry to come to a quiet corner in the classroom.

"Harry, look at me. Do not walk away. Stay and listen when someone talks to you," Willard said.

"It's boring," Harry answered.

"That's okay. This is how you act with people. You stay with them when they want to talk with you."

"I want to read my book about fish," Harry said.

"You can do that later," Willard said. "Now, you are learning to listen to people."

"Only for a few minutes."

"When you listen to someone, you look at them," Willard said. "Look at me."

Harry glanced at his teacher and then looked away.

"That's a good start. Good job. Now, look at me again, and look at me for a count of three. One . . . two . . . three."

Diagnosing Asperger's

This disorder can easily go undiagnosed, especially in milder cases. When people are aware that something is wrong, it is often confused with autism, obsessive-compulsive disorder, and even ADHD. It is currently believed that it occurs more often in boys than in girls.

Most often, a special education teacher or other specialist offers this type of instruction. It is important for you to know about it, however, because there will be many opportunities for you to reinforce your student's social learning in the classroom. In addition, because you see your student in many social situations, you are an excellent observer and can tell his social skills instructor specific areas in which he needs help.

Social Relationship With Peers

Catch your student doing something appropriate in the social arena and praise him for his behavior. If, for example, you've noticed that he's just shared his felt-tip pens with a classmate at the art table, say something like, "That was good that you shared your pens with Maryam." It's interesting to note that, for many kids, we praise by saying, "I like the way you . . ." Since students with Asperger's are not necessarily trying to please you, however, this is a less effective praising technique for them. Also, focusing on what they did right, such as "That was good that you . . . ," reinforces their positive actions.

There may be students in your class who model positive behaviors and are less likely to respond to negative behaviors. As much as possible, place your student with Asperger's near these students. He is working hard at learning the social rules but, until he masters them, try to create as positive and as supportive a social environment as possible.

To help your student stop talking excessively about a topic he is interested in, create a simple cueing system (it can be tapping the side of your hand). This should alert your student that he is talking too much and monopolizing a conversation. Do allow him times in the day, however, when he can focus on his area of interest. This may be an excellent reinforcement for positive behavior.

Structuring the Day

Providing a consistent environment is important for all kids, but your student with Asperger's especially feels safest when his environment stays the same. In the morning, you can announce to the whole class what is going to happen that day, even if it is the same schedule that you always follow.

Transitions

Prepare your student in advance for transitions. This can be as simple as saying, "Harry, we're going to go to lunch in five minutes." If there is a significant change of schedule like an assembly program, take more time to prepare him. A minute of talking about a new activity can prevent a great deal of distress for everyone.

Dealing With Behavior Issues

It's important to remember that your student with Asperger's may not be motivated by the desire to please you. Behavior management should focus on clear expectations and not on emotional appeals. Telling him that you will feel happy if he cleans out his desk will probably have little impact. Students with these issues do, however, follow rules; in fact, they depend on them to help them feel more safe and secure. Create clear and simple expectations for appropriate behavior. Then, with the help of the whole class, turn these into class rules that are written out on a large piece of paper and put in an obvious place in the classroom. Explain the consequences of inappropriate behavior and be absolutely consistent about carrying them out. A good consequence for students with Asperger's is a time-out in a place where there is very little stimulation.

Another big part of behavior management for a student with Asperger's is to recognize the student's strengths. He wants to do well and to fit in, but he often doesn't know how. He doesn't understand what he's doing wrong, and therefore, his sense of self-esteem can be low. Acknowledge his strengths and let them shine. For example, Ruth Spencer's sixth-grade student Ori has an excellent memory for facts. His class has been studying the Constitution, and Ruth knows that Ori has been interested in this subject and developed a true mastery of the information. During the afternoon class discussion, Ruth asks Ori two factual questions that she is sure he knows. Ori feels the satisfaction of being a participating member of the class and of doing something right. He also gets valuable practice in waiting his turn to answer.

Curriculum

Start with the concrete to teach abstract concepts and use as many hands-on activities as you can. Ask your student to tell you, in his own words, what he has learned so far through the activities. Don't be fooled by a recitation of facts. You need to make sure that he understands the underlying basic concepts.

Complex tasks should be broken down into smaller units, and these should be clearly laid out in terms of what needs to be done first, second, and so on. Check to make sure that your student understands what you are asking him to do on a particular academic task. If he has fine motor difficulties, you may need to expect less motor output in classwork and homework, and you may need to give him more time for tests. It can simply take him longer to write.

Be aware of levels of stimulation in your classroom and place your student where he can be most focused on instruction. Since he can be very sensitive to sensory input, he may also have difficulty paying attention, you need to be vigilant about this. If a new sensory stimulation comes into your classroom—for example, an aquarium or a new computer—ask yourself, "Where is he sitting? How will this affect his learning?"

Talking With Your Student

It's hard not to use clichés and idioms because they are so common and pervasive. If you do use one, however, like, "I wouldn't want to be in his shoes," explain it right away. Also, teach your student to tell you when he is truly confused.

Henry DaSilva hadn't read his third-grade student Michael's IEP since the beginning of the year, and in mid-October he thought he should look at it again. Reading the IEP a second time, he realized that Michael actually had a goal that said, "Michael will tell an adult when he is confused about an idiomatic expression." Somehow, seeing the goal in the IEP made it more real. Now, Henry would really pay attention to comments that he or others made around Michael, like, "The answer was as plain as the nose on his face," or "He bought the car for a song." Now Henry knew that when an idiomatic expression came up, he needed to check if Michael appeared confused.

A Short Interview With a Woman Who Teaches Social Skills to Students With Asperger's:

How do you approach this work?
"I tell the kids we're going to be detectives, that people in the world are constantly giving us messages. Sometimes, these messages are in words and they're clear. They'll say, 'Stop doing that.' But people aren't always so good with their words and, sometimes, you have to be a detective to figure out what they really mean. And, lots of times, people give us messages that are conveyed in other ways, like with the ways their faces look."

How do you teach about facial expressions?
"When I teach them to recognize other people's expressions, I start with really clear photographs of people making different faces, and then we connect that with an 'I' statement. 'I'm feeling very sad,' or whatever. Then, I go to drawings, usually cartoon drawings. It works. Role-playing works, too.

We do this fun thing at the end of the unit, when I feel the kids are doing pretty well. I got the idea from somebody else. We go on a facial expression scavenger hunt. We literally go downtown, and everybody has a list of facial expressions they have to find: mad, disappointed, joyful, impatient. The kids really love it."

Do you find that your kids really learn how to relate?
"Yes. Absolutely. Kids with Asperger's are very teachable. They can get it. They can learn."

Do you have a tip for a classroom teacher who has a kid with Asperger's in her class?
"Always remember that they're not trying to irritate you. Hold that thought in your mind."

Tourette Syndrome

Right from the beginning of school, Carlos didn't quite seem to fit into first grade. It was hard for Tony Martinelli to put his finger on what exactly was wrong, but Carlos got upset easily, usually on the way to lunch or recess, and especially when the hall was crowded with other kids.

In the classroom, Carlos held bunches of pencils and crayons in his fist. Then, he would suddenly let them go and watch them fall. Carlos blinked a lot, and occasionally, out of nowhere, he would pound his feet on the floor.

One Wednesday afternoon, Carlos started flapping his arms and hands. The other kids made a joke of it and said that Carlos was acting like a bird. Carlos didn't laugh, however, but ran out of the room. Tony found him sitting against the school building in the alley.

"I'm sorry," Carlos said. "I can't stop."

"I know. I've seen you try to stop," Tony said. "Don't you worry. We're going to get you some help."

Tony called Carlos's parents and, together, they made a referral for an evaluation. The evaluation determined that Carlos had Tourette Syndrome.

What is Tourette Syndrome?

A person with Tourette (or Tourette's) Syndrome (TS), displays fast and repetitive movements called tics. People with TS may have a limited amount of control over their tics for a limited time. The tics do, however, need to be released, and the longer they are held in, the more severe they get. Researchers currently believe Tourette Syndrome is an inherited disorder, caused by a chemical imbalance in the brain.

At present, there is no medical test for the disorder. A person is diagnosed as having TS if the following are present:

❋ lots of motor tics

❋ vocal tics

❋ variations in the types and severity of tics from one day to the next (or hour to hour)

❋ onset of tics in childhood (between ages 2 and 18), mostly occurring at 6 or 7 years of age

(Adapted from Conners, 2002)

What are some unique characteristics of students with Tourette Syndrome?

Symptoms vary in levels of severity. Most people with TS have a mild to moderate form of the disorder. There are two main kinds of tics: motor and vocal. Motor tics can occur in any part of the body and may be simple or complex. Heather, a fourth-grader, has a simple tic where she grimaces unexpectedly at people. Another child, Ignacio, taps his fingers excessively. Pam, a third-grader, displays a complex tic in which she coughs twice, taps her feet, and then touches her hands to her shoulders, always in that order.

Vocal tics are the repetition of sounds, words, or groups of words. Here again, vocal tics may be simple, as with Harry, a sixth-grader, who will unexpectedly begin to clear his throat. Complex vocal tics involve repeating groups of words. Repeating inappropriate comments or language is known as *coprolalia*. Fortunately, this is a less common type of vocal tic.

Negative stress, positive excitement, and fatigue make tics more frequent and severe. Tics also may change, especially with children, making classroom life especially challenging. You can spend lots of time and energy trying to figure out coping strategies for one tic, only to realize it has suddenly been replaced by a new one. Patience and understanding are critical.

If there is no intervention, students with TS can experience serious difficulties with their peers. Consider Jason, for example, a fifth-grader who will suddenly turn to a peer at lunch and say, "You're skinny. You're too skinny." Cathy, a second-grader, will jump up and hop around her desk and then sit on the floor and bang her legs together.

Kids with TS frequently have other challenges, such as ADHD, learning disabilities (especially nonverbal learning disabilities), and obsessive-compulsive disorder (OCD). In the past, students with TS have been misdiagnosed as having only one or more of these other issues, and the TS has been overlooked. The most common issue to occur with TS is OCD. In OCD, a person has difficulty controlling his thoughts. He feels compelled to do certain things (a compulsion) in order to relieve the anxiety caused by the repetitive thought or fear (the obsession).

TOURETTE SYNDROME

What does my student with Tourette Syndrome need from me?

Understanding Your Student

Understanding the disorder is the single most important factor in working with a child with TS. Because of the unsettling nature of his behavior, he is often judged negatively. Teachers (even good, kind teachers) can almost feel the words, "Why can't you just *stop*," on their lips. Don't say them. They don't help. But don't blame yourself for wanting to say them, either. Just understand that your student is not misbehaving. He just can't make himself stop. He can work at holding back certain behaviors for limited periods of time, but he simply can't stop. And if he gets upset or feels frightened or tired, his tics will probably get worse.

Social Relationships With Peers

Your student not only needs your understanding, but also the understanding of his peers. To this end, the most helpful thing you can do is educate your whole class, as long as the special education team, your student, and your student's parents agree. Everyone needs to accept and endorse what is going to be done. The education needs to be done with great sensitivity. TS, however, is not a subtle, hidden disorder that can be quietly ignored, and without education of peers, your student with TS is less likely to have friends and feel like he is a valued member of the class. An excellent educational program called *Educating Classmates About Tourette Syndrome (A Peer In-Service)* is available on the Internet at www.tsa-usa.org

Dealing With Behavior

Understanding TS is the first step. Finding creative ways to handle tics and related problems is the second. The peacefulness of your classroom environment needs to be protected not only for the other students but also for the child with Tourette. The simplest and easiest thing to do is to allow the child to take frequent breaks from the large group so he can relax and release any tics he's been holding in.

Some people recommend allowing the student with TS to go to the bathroom or to get frequent drinks at the water fountain. Others recommend dealing directly with the issue and openly acknowledging that your student needs to be in a private space occasionally. If he has only motor tics, perhaps privacy could be created in the classroom by putting a divider diagonally in a back corner of the classroom. If the tics are vocal, you will need to establish a safe place outside of the classroom. Ask the special education teacher for help with this. There may be a small area that could be set aside for your student.

Some tics are simply not acceptable in a classroom environment and, for students who have them, frequent breaks are not the answer. This is where you need to be extremely creative in finding ways to cope. Mary Glowacki's second-grade student Patty would suddenly turn to a nearby person and bite him or her. Mary talked with Patty and asked the other kids for suggestions, too. Patty suggested that she keep an apple in her pocket to grab and bite whenever she felt the urge to bite someone. It worked. Patty needed to get up and go to a private spot pretty quickly, but she was able to chomp on the fruit rather than a person. She and everyone else were much happier.

Amy Foster's seventh-grade student Gregory suddenly began shouting nonsense syllables while jumping up high and then landing down hard. Gregory was not able to stop this complex tic, even though he had been successful at holding in other tics until he could release them in private spaces. Amy first learned of this particular behavior when the bus driver reported it. The frequency of the tic then escalated, especially on the bus, and at lunch and recess. Gregory was a popular boy and his peers developed a unique way of dealing with this tic: they began copying his behaviors. This helped Gregory not to feel so embarrassed, but it also terrified the younger children in the school. Here was this group of rather large boys shouting in a strange way while jumping erratically. Amy met with Gregory and his peers and discussed the issue. First, she complimented the group on the creativity and compassion they had shown. They were, after all, trying to help Gregory. She then asked the boys if they had noticed how the other, especially younger kids, had seemed to react. When they acknowledged that they'd noticed that the other kids seemed scared, she asked if they could think of a different way of handling the situation. Gregory himself came up with the solution. He suggested that if this tic occurred again, one of his friends should stand nearby and make sure that he was safe when he landed and that he wouldn't hurt anyone else. The friend could tell the other kids that Gregory was okay and that he just needed to do this. The group tried this compensatory strategy, and it worked quite well.

Structuring the Day

Since students with TS are often more stressed in nonstructured situations such as lunch, recess, and on the school bus, and in crowded situations, such as assembly programs, be especially aware during these times.

Once again, think creatively. For example, you might visit the auditorium with your student, show him where your class usually sits, and ask him where he would feel most comfortable. Sitting in the last seat in a row, next to you might be good. He can take a break from the program without too much notice from the other kids. If the hallways in your school are crowded and busy, it might be best to leave the classroom a few minutes before or after the other kids do.

Tests

Allow your student with TS to take tests in a private space without time limits. Taking tests, in general, is an anxiety-producing situation. Alex, a sixth grader, gets very nervous taking tests, and when he gets nervous, he barks quite loudly. This makes his peers angry, and this makes Alex more nervous because he's embarrassed and then he barks even more. Soon his ability to concentrate on the test is completely gone. It's far better to find a private place where Alex can take the test and bark when he needs to. Without time limits, he'll relax even more.

Curriculum

Many students with TS have difficulties with fine motor and visual motor functioning. For this reason, some homework and classroom assignments need to be shorter, since handwriting can be laborious. In many cases, the use of a word processor is helpful. Check with the special education team to see if an occupational therapy evaluation is indicated. An occupational therapist can provide many helpful suggestions for daily classroom work.

A Final Note

Since many students with TS also have other challenges, especially the ones listed below, please refer to the following pages for information and specific suggestions on how to help your student.

Learning Disabilities: pages 14–32
ADHD: pages 38–44
Emotional Disturbances: pages 102–109

Check your student's IEP to see which specific goals he may have that relate to one or more of these areas. Andrea's Wellen's fifth-grade student Henry, for example, has ADHD in addition to having TS. One of Henry's goals is, "Henry will be able to create a written plan of the steps needed to complete a multistep task." When Andrea assigns such a task—for example, a science report—she needs to check that Henry has been able to complete his plan. If he hasn't, she either helps him with it or asks the special education teacher to do so.

Mentale Retardation

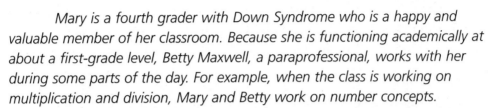

Mary is a fourth grader with Down Syndrome who is a happy and valuable member of her classroom. Because she is functioning academically at about a first-grade level, Betty Maxwell, a paraprofessional, works with her during some parts of the day. For example, when the class is working on multiplication and division, Mary and Betty work on number concepts.

Mary loves books and will spend lots of time carefully looking at them. At first, she related only to books with minimal text but now will attend to the text and follow along as someone reads to her.

Mary discovered a favorite book when Betty first read Dr. Desoto *by William Steig (Farrar, Straus and Giroux, 1982) to her. Mary requested this story so much, that she actually memorized much of the text.*

During the week, there are times when students are asked to read to each other. Because so many of the kids enjoy Dr. Desoto, *they ask Mary to read it to them. All of the kids greatly enjoy this special time.*

What is mental retardation?

According to the Association of Retarded Citizens (ARC), a diagnosis of mental retardation is based on three criteria:

* The person must score below 70 on an IQ test.
* The person must have serious limitations in at least two areas of adaptive living skills (skills such as self-care, the ability to self-direct, academic functioning, and communication).
* The impairment must be present from childhood (18 years or younger).

Before the age of nine, kids with these characteristics are referred to as developmentally delayed. After age nine, they are referred to as having intellectual impairment.

What are some unique characteristics of students with mental retardation?

People with mental retardation are all very different from one another, with varying strengths and weaknesses. The great majority of them are only somewhat slower than the total school population in acquiring new concepts and skills. About 13 percent, the people with recorded IQs under 50, have more significant challenges.

People go through stages of development. As described by the child psychologist Jean Piaget, the typical stages are as follows:

❉ From birth through age two, children primarily use sensory and motor activities to learn about the world.

❉ From age two to age six, they begin to use intuition and language.

❉ From age seven to age eleven, they develop logical thinking skills. In this stage, it's important for them to have physical objects that they can practice ordering and organizing.

❉ At 12 years and older, people think more abstractly and can hypothesize and predict what will happen.

For kids with mental retardation, it's important to focus on their level of development as opposed to their chronological age.

Kids with mental retardation also have different types of intelligences, as do all people. Howard Gardner, in his book *Frames of Mind: The Theory of Multiple Intelligences* (Basic Books, 1993), proposes that there are seven different types of intelligences (listed in the box at right).

Your student may have a relative strength in her bodily-kinesthetic intelligence and learn best when given hands-on materials to manipulate and the freedom to move around in the classroom environment, rather than having to sit for extended periods of time. She may also have strength in her musical intelligence, so songs and rhythms may help her remember certain facts and ideas.

Some kids with mental retardation require other types of services in addition to careful curriculum planning, such as speech therapy, occupational therapy, and physical therapy. Some need a different physical education program, called adaptive physical education.

Gardner's Multiple Intelligences

❉ linguistic (the ability to learn and remember language)

❉ logical-mathematical (the ability to figure things out and discover patterns)

❉ spatial (the ability to be aware of and correctly judge spatial relationships)

❉ bodily-kinesthetic (the ability to enjoy and learn well through movement)

❉ musical (the ability to relate to tunes and rhythms)

❉ interpersonal (the ability to get along well with others)

❉ intrapersonal (a high degree of self-awareness and understanding)

What does my student with mental retardation need from me?

Understanding Your Student

Kids with mental retardation often lack confidence. Even before she got to school, your student may have faced problems learning skills such as feeding herself, walking, and talking. She may have faced silent or overt disapproval from adults and other kids. You may hear your student say, "No," or "I don't know," to every question asked of her in class. You may see her look away when she thinks you might ask her a question, or ask to go to the bathroom when a new area of learning is being presented. Your student may focus her energies on not failing rather than on risking a mistake. She wants to stay safe. Praise her for her attempts and successes and make light of mistakes. Sometimes it helps if you purposely make an obvious mistake and then very dramatically, with lightness and humor, say, "I made a mistake. Oh, well. Everyone makes mistakes."

Know that your student needs to be a valuable, contributing member of the class. To help this happen, first ask yourself, "What are her strengths? Are there any barriers to her succeeding with any given task?" Rick Hillager's kindergarten student Tanya has significant delays with speech. She is just beginning to speak in sentences. How can Tanya contribute in the classroom? Rick noticed that Tanya loves to look at pictures. She sits quietly and is attentive whenever he reads a picture book to the class. Tanya follows directions when she is prepared for them and is given the opportunity to practice. So Rick took Tanya aside and taught her to hold the book he was reading, to keep it open to the page he had just read, and to show the page to her classmates. Once Tanya had done this for the class, he asked the other kids if they wanted to do the same thing. Tanya became a part of the community of kids who were read-aloud helpers.

Curriculum

Learn about your student's developmental level and types of intelligence so you can plan how to include her in learning activities. Then, structure your lessons carefully. Think about the steps involved and present skills and concepts to her sequentially. Ahead of time, plan how you will evaluate her learning. Ask yourself, "What do I want my student to be able to do when the lesson is over?" It's okay if the skill or concept she is working on is different from what the other students are working on, as long as she receives instruction at her developmental level.

Always review what has been presented before, and take your time as you introduce new information. Then practice, practice, practice and review. Your student will need a lot of reinforcement. Games and computers can provide some of this. Depth of learning rather than breadth is important to help her remain confident that she can learn.

When you present information, use as many different cues as possible, such as visual, tactile, and kinesthetic. Concrete materials help a lot. Your student will be more interested and engaged when there is an object to feel and hold and move. This is easier to do with mathematics, but it can be effective with other subjects also.

If your class is studying a country in social studies, for example, it makes sense to let the kids hold objects unique to that country, or to ask people who know music from the country to come in and sing or play a song.

Create situations where your student is an active learner rather than a passive one. For example, your second-grade student Beth already knows the name of the letter *b*, and you are now teaching her its sound. Provide a lowercase model of the letter. Then, write four words that begin with *b* on a large piece of paper. You could write *bat*, *bell*, *bed* and *bear*. Here's a sample dialogue:

Teacher: What do you notice about all these words?

Beth: They're all short.

Teacher: Very good. What else do you notice about them?

Beth: They start with that letter, the letter *b*.

Teacher: Yes, it is a *b*. Now listen closely. (Point to each word as you say it.) What sound does each word start with?

Beth: /b/

Teacher: Excellent. Let's do it again. [Say each word a second time.] What sound does each word start with?

Beth: /b/

Teacher: Yes, so what sound does the letter *b* make?

Beth: /b/

You: Nice job.

You didn't tell Beth what sound *b* makes. You created a situation where she discovered it for herself. This will help her maintain interest and remember her new learning.

When teaching a concept, focus on that one concept and try to eliminate distracting elements. For example, if you are teaching the number concept of "four," have groups of four things that are the same, like four red blocks, rather than different colored blocks. Make learning relate to your student's life experience as much as possible. For math word problems, for example, create problems that use your student's name or the name of one of her friends and that relate directly to her life. Creating these types of word problems can be a great writing activity for all the students in your class. You can select or write appropriate ones for your student with mental retardation.

Make yourself familiar with instructional tools. There are many companies that offer excellent materials that can help. Lindamood-Bell (www.lblp.com) offers materials for language arts. These can be ordered through Gander Publishing (www.ganderpublishing.com; 800-554-1819). An interesting math program is TouchMath (www.touchmath.com; 800-888-9191). Attainment Company (www.attainmentcompany.com; 800-327-4269) offers a wide variety of curriculum materials for kids with special needs.

Computers can be valuable. Find software that will offer opportunities for reinforcement of skills. If you find the right software, your student will gain hours of valuable practice time—and she will enjoy using it.

Talking With Your Student

Give your student plenty of time to answer questions. She may need more time to process information. Also, kids with mental retardation can be nervous about making a mistake, and your student may be hoping that, while she is silent, you or another student will jump in with the answer. You need to make it clear that everyone will have all the time they need to answer. Your job, as a teacher, is to guard this quiet thinking time.

Dealing With Behavior

Use praise as much as possible to help your student behave well in your classroom. When she is acting inappropriately, tell her to stop, and clearly and calmly tell her what the problem is. Tell her what she needs to do instead. Praise is the most effective behavior modifier for kids with mental retardation. Time-out and punishment don't work nearly as well. So watch for when your student is acting well, and praise, praise, praise.

Expectations

Expect your student to accomplish what she is capable of doing. In the past, others may have focused on what she couldn't do and may have done things for her that she could have done for herself. Very directly encourage her to try. She needs your support, but she *can* become more and more independent.

When Rosa Rodriguez's third-grade class was preparing to go on a field trip, her student Carl stood silently, holding out his raincoat to her.

"My mom always helps me with the buttons," he told her.

"I think you can do them yourself," Rosa answered. "The buttons are only a little bigger than the ones on your jacket."

"Ms. Evans [his second-grade teacher] always helped me," Carl said.

"You're in third grade now," Rosa said. "Here, let me watch you as you do one."

While it would have been easier for Rosa to quickly button Carl's raincoat, he benefits more by becoming independent.

Homework and Tests

Evaluate your student's progress by observing how she functions in class rather than using test scores on homework assignments. Homework is important, but make sure it provides good practice for things she has already learned at school. Your student will benefit from homework most if she can complete it independently at home. It will be most effective if her parents understand what she is supposed to do and if they know how to prompt her to complete the task successfully. Don't use homework as a way to challenge her. She needs work that she can be successful with when she's tired after a long day at school. Keep the homework pages simple, without a lot of extra text. For math problems, put only a few on a page.

> ### *Common Causes of Mental Retardation*
>
> There are hundreds of causes of mental retardation, some known and others unknown at this time. The three most common ones that we know about are:
>
> - Fragile X syndrome (a gene disorder on the X chromosome)
> - Down syndrome (a chromosomal disorder)
> - Fetal alcohol syndrome (caused by the excessive use of alcohol by a pregnant mother)

Social Relationships With Peers

If other kids want to, let them participate in your student's learning. Other kids may enjoy playing games, doing drills, or reading books with your student. This offers not only a great deal of practice time for everyone, but it also helps create a warm and friendly social environment.

Relating to Parents

Communication between school and home is very important. Parents need to know what their child is studying so they can reinforce learning, and teachers need to know if there are any special issues that are coming up at home. A good vehicle for this communication is a home-school notebook, which the child carries back and forth. Celebrate successes in this book, so that your student will be proud and happy to bring it home. A daily checklist that requests specific information from the family may also be helpful.

An Interview With a Person Who Works With People With Mental Retardation

"The problem with these terms, like Down Syndrome, is that the framework becomes that this is a Down Syndrome kid. We should refer to people as people first: a kid with Down Syndrome, not a Down Syndrome kid.

"The implication is that all kids with Down Syndrome are alike. It's like saying that all kids with red hair are alike. I've known hundreds of people with Down Syndrome, and they're as different from each other as people without Down Syndrome are.

"A person with mental retardation is often described as a person who 'can't.' I know people with mental retardation, adults, who have their own houses, drive cars, have children. I go out to lunch once in a while with a man who was institutionalized as a child and lived there most of his adult life. Now, he's got his own apartment and he has his own life. He is happy about so many things. I go out to lunch with him because I like to. I admire him."

Gifted and Talented

When Roland entered kindergarten, Eleanor Cummings saw an active little boy who would suddenly stand up and run in circles around the room. Roland also had an amazing ability with mathematics, both with computation and mathematical reasoning. He loved numbers and would talk about math with anyone who would listen.

One afternoon, Eleanor overheard him at the farm play station. "Look," he said to a friend. "There are three horses and three cows and three pigs and three chickens. That means there are four groups of three: twelve animals."

Eleanor called Roland's parents. "Who taught him this?" she asked.

"No one," Roland's mom answered. "A couple of years ago, Roland just got so interested in math, he started figuring out things for himself. Last year, he asked me how many days it was until his birthday. I told him it was twelve weeks."

"Oh, seven times twelve," Roland said, "that's too hard for me to figure out. But wait a minute. Ten times seven is seventy, and two times seven is fourteen. Eighty-four days until my birthday. Right, Mom? I'll be four in eighty-four days."

Eleanor contacted the special education team at her school. They arranged for a retired math teacher who enjoyed working with gifted kids to come into the kindergarten to work with Roland.

Sometimes, Roland still ran around the room and often he had a lot of trouble sitting still. But he loved his special math buddy, and he loved being in kindergarten.

What is gifted and talented?

A person may be gifted and/or talented in the following ability areas: intellectual, creative, artistic, leadership, and/or a specific academic area. To be called gifted and/or talented, a person does not have to be a high achiever; rather, he needs only the potential to become so. Also, the definition of giftedness is no longer limited to having a high IQ. According to the National Association for Gifted Children (NAGC), approximately 5 percent, or three million children in the United States are gifted and/or talented.

The federal government does not mandate special education services for children who are gifted and/or talented. It encourages states to set up services for them, but the final decisions are left up to local governments.

What are some unique characteristics of students who are gifted and/or talented?

The identification of gifted kids can be difficult. Even though the definition of gifted is no longer limited to having an IQ of 130–135 or higher, most people still think of gifted children in this way. Since IQ scores can be influenced by opportunity and expectations, gifted kids tend to be identified more often in middle- and upper-class neighborhoods. Unfortunately, many truly gifted children in less privileged neighborhoods are not identified. Sometimes, these kids hide their gifts from their peers because they want to fit in.

The identification of kids with talents may also be difficult. Kids with talents show particular potential in three main areas: creative pursuits such as the visual or performing arts, leadership, and athletics. These are often observed early in the child's life, but only if there has been exposure to the ability area. Therefore, cultural factors can also play a large role in the identification of these kids and their unique abilities.

If cultural issues and class issues influence the identification of a gifted and/or talented student, how can you, as a classroom teacher, know who they are? Sometimes, they are high achievers but sometimes they are not. You may have to rely on other guideposts.

Gifted kids ask a lot of questions. They're curious, always eager to know why and how. They're not satisfied with just the facts. They think abstractly, and enjoy solving complex problems.

Gifted kids like to create their own processes for solving problems, often coming up with unique and different solutions. They may not be correct, but they're in there, thinking about the problem and experimenting. They are self-directed learners who avidly pursue areas of interest. They often prefer to work independently but enjoy exchanging ideas, often with adults or older peers. Sometimes, one idea leads to another that leads to another.

Gifted and talented kids can have uneven development. For example, Juan, a third grader, is advanced in language skills and vocabulary, but his physical development, particularly his fine motor development, is what one would expect of a boy his chronological age. He became very interested in the universe and understood many complex concepts. He felt great frustration, however, when he tried to build a model of our solar system but couldn't get his hands to do the intricate work.

There are stereotypes about the social and emotional lives of gifted and talented kids. All of us have heard stories about the skinny boy who is brilliant in math but who is constantly teased on the school bus because he doesn't relate well to his peers. Every gifted and talented child is an individual with his own set of strengths and weaknesses just like everyone else. Some are socially adept, and some are not.

Gifted kids are frequently very sensitive, however. They tend to demand perfection of themselves. This can make them afraid of failure and may encourage a fear of trying. They know they can do well by performing at the level that is easy for them, but fear failing if they attempt something more challenging. It's possible that so many skills and concepts have come so easily to them that they haven't learned how to handle frustration and failure in academic areas. Also, their heightened awareness of what is going on around them makes them particularly sensitive to the potential for failure. Being wrong feels really hard.

Some gifted and talented kids can have special needs, and this can complicate the identification of their areas of special strengths. They may have learning disabilities, ADHD, or physical limitations, just like the rest of the school population.

What does my student who is gifted and/or talented need from me?

Social Relationships With Peers

The emotional climate of your classroom is critically important to your student's comfort and success. Like all other kids with special needs, he needs to feel like a regular kid who is a valued member of the group. Recognize and acknowledge your student's gifts or talents to him privately, but don't make it a big deal in front of the other kids in the class. Unfortunately, in our culture, very bright or talented people are sometimes thought of as odd. The other kids will know that he has a special strength, but if this is accepted as "normal" for him and not fussed over, it will help the other kids relate to him better.

Curriculum

Even if your student has already mastered much of the material that will be covered in your classroom this year, he still has academic needs. If he's not challenged, he'll feel that school is boring and that he doesn't have to pay attention or put forth any effort or creativity. He needs to learn that his unique gifts are valued, and that he's going to have to work to develop them.

When you are beginning an area of instruction, quickly assess whether your student already has the concepts and skills that are going to be addressed. If he does, have an alternative plan for instruction. For example, if your student understands and can use the concept of place value, don't ask him to complete the same worksheets that most other kids are doing. Rather, he might like to write several story problems that involve place value. Later, these might be shared with some other kids in class.

Betty O'Mara's fourth-grade student Allen got 19 correct on the regular Monday pretest for the 20-word spelling test. Betty asked Allen to select a few words from the book he was reading that he'd like to learn to spell, and she selected some, too. When he got 2 words correct out of 20, Betty knew this was the list for him to study.

While drill work benefits some children, it is ultimately destructive to have a child do highly repetitive drill work in areas where he has already achieved mastery. It's fair to ask a child to do drill work if he needs it. Most kids need to use flash cards to practice their multiplication tables, for example. But if a student already knows these tables, it's not fair to ask him to do this work. If there is a sound intellectual reason for the drill work, your student will usually accept it and complete the task willingly. If not, however, he may become angry because his sense of justice has been violated.

> ### A Quick Tip
>
> A great way to gain information about your student's interests (and all your other kids' interests) is to have your whole class complete an interest inventory. Even if you need to develop special projects for your student in the subject area that the class is studying (not an established interest for him yet), you can still get help from his interest inventory.

In some schools, the philosophy is that the gifted student can have different assignments, but that they should be in the same area of study as what the class is working on. In other schools, the student is free to pursue his own interests. Speak with your principal and the student and his parents to determine which approach you need to use.

75

Alfred Robert's sixth grade is studying ancient Egypt, and he knows that his student Ron is fascinated by the topic of transportation. Alfred challenged Ron to find out as much as he could about the ways people and materials got around. Alfred also knows that Ron is very interested in current events and government. Alfred asked Ron to create a page of a newspaper that might have been published in ancient Egypt.

Sometimes, the other kids may ask why your gifted student gets to do special activities. A good way to respond to this is to say that he is doing the type of learning activity that he needs, just like every other person in the class. It *is* important to make sure that in general the "fun level" of all activities seems equitable.

For gifted kids who read quickly and well, get help from your school and/or local librarian. It can be a challenge to find age-appropriate books for some kids. Lorna Mancini's second-grade student Maria reads at a seventh-grade reading level. Maria doesn't want or need to be reading about complex preteen relationship issues, or other topics of interest to 12-year-olds. Maria is very interested in history. The school librarian recommended the *Dear America* series by Scholastic. The books have fascinating historical information, are age appropriate for a second grader, and best of all, are a series—which means there are lots of them. Maria loved them and got lots of special project ideas from each one.

You don't have to think up projects on your own; your student can come up with great ideas, too. When the ideas are proposed, think about the areas you feel your student can profit from working in. Perhaps he is a good creative writer but hasn't written nonfiction in a long time, for example. Also, keep the projects varied so that he gains practice in many different areas.

Sometimes, gifted and talented kids can also have learning or other issues. When Roberta Pignatto checked her fourth-grade student Ellen's IEP, she learned that Ellen, who was amazingly aware of current events and who exhibited intellectual curiosity in many ways, had Tourette Syndrome. It was a mild case, but now Roberta knew that she needed to speak with the special education teacher not only about Ellen's gifts, but also about how to support her as she learned how to deal with Tourette Syndrome.

Talking With Your Student

Be careful with praise. An artist named Thaddeus reports that his drawing was almost ruined by praise when he was a child. He drew well, in a far more sophisticated way than his peers, and his accomplishment was so obvious that adults praised him effusively. As a child, he believed that everything he drew was perfect and he had no more to learn about drawing. What they needed to do, Thaddeus reports, was to say, "Oh, very nice. You've worked hard on that drawing." And then they needed to find an art mentor or instructor who could help him truly develop his skills.

Relating to Parents

Your student's parents can be great advocates for your student. Speak with them about any issues or needs that arise and see if they are able to offer suggestions or help.

A Short Interview With a Young Woman Who Is Gifted in Reading and Writing

What was school like for you when you were a kid?
"In fourth grade, it was hard. The teacher would hand out something for the whole class to read, and then I'd read it and sit there, and then she'd tell me to read it again. She didn't believe I could read it that fast. Once, she made me read a whole book again."

Do you remember any teacher doing something that really helped you?
"My fifth-grade teacher was awesome. I'll never forget her. She had this bulletin board all decorated, and there were envelopes stuck on with ideas for projects. When anybody finished their work, they could go to the board and check out the envelopes and see if they wanted to do something. In one of them, there was a description of the Molasses Tragedy. Do you know about that?"

Oh, you mean that time in Boston in 1919 when the huge tank of molasses exploded and flooded the neighborhood.
"Yes, it killed people. It was terrible. Well, I'd just read about it, and the project that I liked best was to write about how I imagined the people would have cleaned up the molasses. But then the fun part was to write about how we'd clean it up now, and how we'd clean up in the future. Those envelopes with those ideas were like treasures. I thought of all those envelopes as treasures."

Partial Hearing Loss and Deafness

Telly lost her hearing at nine years of age when she was visiting her brother who was working on a construction site. She wore a hard hat, but it didn't offer enough protection from an accidental explosion. Telly seemed to adjust well at first. She responded to her speech therapy because she had heard sounds for the first years of her life, and she was doing well with lip-reading skills.

In fifth grade, however, Telly suddenly appeared unmotivated and depressed. The other kids liked Telly a lot and tried to reach out, but she withdrew from her friends, saying it was too hard to talk. After school, Telly stopped playing soccer and just went home and played with her dog.

Then Telly's friend Yoshi made an important discovery. One morning, when Telly got to school, Yoshi was there waiting with a special book, Sound Friendships: The Story of Willa and Her Hearing Ear Dog *by Elizabeth Yates (Countryman Press, 1987).*

"Willa, the girl in the story, she lost her hearing when she was ten because a firecracker went off right next to her ear," Yoshi said. "She's grown-up in the book. She has a dog, a hearing-ear dog, and her dog, Honey, lets her know about any sounds, like the doorbell ringing or the fire alarm going off. Maybe you could get a hearing-ear dog."

Telly shook her head. "No," she said. "It's just for grown-ups."

"Well, maybe. You'll be grown-up someday. And maybe you can find out about it. You love dogs. It would be so cool. You could go anywhere with him—the movies, the gym."

Telly took the book and walked away. Later that morning when the class had some free time, Yoshi saw her on the computer. There was a picture of a dog on the screen. Telly smiled as Yoshi walked by.

What is partial hearing loss and deafness?

Partial hearing loss is the impaired ability to hear sounds. This loss can be permanent or intermittent. Deafness is a significant hearing impairment. There are various degrees of impairment, determined by how much a person hears with amplification. Another factor to consider is not only how well a student is hearing sounds, but also how much she is understanding speech sounds. The Alexander Graham Bell Association for the Deaf and Hard of Hearing Web site, www.agbell.org, contains a great deal of information about the types of hearing loss and their effects.

What are some unique characteristics of students who have a partial hearing loss or who are deaf?

Hearing loss affects not only verbal communication but also reading and other language-based skills. The student who has never heard language is affected the most severely.

Even with a hearing aid that is effective, it is estimated that many students pick up only 60 to 70 percent of spoken language. Screening out background noises can be very difficult. A mother of a child who is deaf explained this best when she said, "People have the misconception that if you put on a hearing aid, you can hear. But you don't hear as well because acuity and auditory discrimination are not as good. Also, a lot of kids, especially little kids, don't like wearing them because they're uncomfortable and some of them don't really work. Once, my son buried his hearing aid in the backyard!"

Intermittent, also called "fluctuating," hearing loss can also be very challenging because no one may be aware that the hearing loss is happening. Thus, appropriate modifications are not made, and students can lose valuable information. Intermittent hearing loss is especially influential between the age of birth and three years when children are first learning language.

Students with hearing difficulties are as smart as other kids and there is no correlation between hearing loss and intelligence. They sometimes do, however, have other challenges such as learning disabilities, and a student should be tested if you see signs of other concerns.

Students with hearing loss can have difficulty with auditory discrimination, or hearing the slight differences between sounds. This can greatly affect language meaning; for example, these students might not differentiate the vowel sounds in the words *bat*, *bit*, *bet*, and *but*. This makes it difficult for them to understand spoken language. What's more, in conversational speech, most people speak quickly. If a student is already having trouble with "perfect" English because of difficulty with auditory discrimination, understanding more relaxed conversational speech becomes doubly hard.

Abstract words, such as prepositions, can be confusing. For example, why do we get *in* a car but *on* a bus? And then there are those idiomatic expressions. For example, what does "It's raining cats and dogs" mean? Or, "He's driving me up the wall"? Or, "It was a piece of cake"?

All of these communication issues can contribute to or even create social difficulties. Being the only kid with a hearing difficulties in a classroom can be hard. When Anthony entered fourth grade in a new school, his peers with normal hearing had lots of misconceptions about how they were supposed to relate to him. They thought they were supposed to speak slowly and loudly and to exaggerate certain words. They were trying to make Anthony feel welcome, but their focus on communication difficulties made him feel isolated and angry. Anthony wanted to be a regular kid. He wanted his peers to focus on his needs, wants, and feelings. He wanted to be friends with them.

> ### An Issue
>
> The issue of whether or not students who are deaf should learn a manual language such as ASL is a huge one in the deaf community. Some people strongly believe that deaf children will only become fully functional members of society if they learn to lip read and speak (the oral approach). They feel that learning manual language harms this learning. Other people believe that ASL and languages like it are beautiful and sophisticated languages that offer people a wide range of fluent communication possibilities, and that access to them should not be denied.

Communication issues may create academic problems in school. Writing can be challenging because a common way of internalizing rules of grammar is to hear them. Also, it can be difficult to get verb tenses right, especially when the verbs are irregular, such as *eat* and *ate* or *freeze* and *froze*.

By third or fourth grade, abstract language becomes more important in school, especially in reading. In the transition from third grade to fourth, students are expected to read for meaning. Thus, a difficulty with abstract language, another common issue for students with hearing loss, can affect reading comprehension.

What does my student who has a partial hearing loss or who is deaf need from me?

Communicating With Your Student

If your student can hear and understand some or all of your speech, it is important to speak clearly and at a normal volume and pace. Don't exaggerate words, but try not to slur them together either.

Never turn your back while you are speaking to your student. If an interpreter is present, speak to the student, not the interpreter. Also, create some sort of visual cueing system that allows your student to signal you if she does not understand what is happening. If you are wearing a microphone and you ask a question of the class, pass the mic to whomever answers the question. Your student needs to hear you *and* her peers.

If you wish to call on her to answer a question, first check with the special education team to make sure this is appropriate. If it is, establish a visual cueing system so that your student will know that you are asking a question of her and that you expect an answer. You could simply stand in front of her and tap your hand.

Check with your student's parents about any use of sign. This is very important because some parents want their child to be exposed only to oral language. If parents approve, learn and use basic signs (*sit down, pay attention, stop, happy, sad, help,* and *understand?*) with your student who is deaf. Also, if parents approve, learn to use finger spelling. Finger spelling can be particularly effective with nouns, especially proper nouns like names. Check with your special education team to find out where you can learn these techniques in your area. Also, parents may know of an organization or person who might be willing to come to your school to teach you some signs and finger spelling.

One of your students may be learning to lip read. Melvin Phillip's third-grade student Annie has an IEP goal that says, "Annie will become more comfortable with lip reading." One of her objectives, designed to help her pay closer attention to what the other person is saying, is "Annie will watch the person talking to her as the person speaks." Melvin lets Annie know that when he is speaking with her, he expects her to look at his face closely until he is finished. He tries to keep his sentences short, but he's very clear about asking Annie to exert real effort to pay attention.

Setting Up the Classroom

Be aware of the noise level in your classroom. Carpet can cut down on noise. Have your student sit in a place where there is the least amount of

> ### Sign Language
>
> American Sign Language (ASL) is a manual, visual language that is used in the deaf community in the United States. It does not merely translate the English language into a visual form. It is a unique language with its own grammatical structure.
>
> In finger spelling, every letter is created by a finger formation. These letters are then combined sequentially into words.

background noise. Be aware of unusual sounds. For example, if you were showing a film, it would be counterproductive to place your student near the projector, because the hum of the machine will drown out any sounds you wish her to hear.

Asking your class to form small groups may create a noise problem for your student with a hearing aid. If your students are supposed to discuss topics with one another, that's a lot of voices speaking at once. If, on the other hand, small groups are doing hands-on projects, this is not as distracting, since ongoing conversation is not occurring. Be aware of where your student's group is placed. It would be best to have her group in the quietest spot possible. Check in with her to see how she's doing in the group.

Structuring the Day

During physical education or in games at recess, make sure your student is aware of the game rules ahead of time. Yelling during the game won't help. Your student also needs to understand the rules and systems of lunch and recess.

There should be a plan in place for your student during fire drills, and check if there is a warning-light system for your deaf student in the classroom and the restrooms.

Curriculum

Use visual cues to reinforce concepts and facts you present in your lessons. If you are showing a film, provide close captioning or a written

Two Special Tips

⊙ Check your student's hearing aid in the morning, and periodically observe her to see if she is acting like it is on. A child, especially a young child, will sometimes turn her hearing aid off because she can be uncomfortable wearing it. She has to learn how to process the sounds her hearing aid gives her, and this can be challenging. Have batteries on hand for the hearing aid.

⊙ Be aware of how auditory cues influence the behavior of people with normal hearing. For example, at the water faucet in your science activity center, the sound of the water still running can remind your students with regular hearing to turn it off. Your student with hearing loss may not have access to these sounds and may have to be taught other ways to remember.

script for your student who can read. Also, provide written directions on the board or at her desk for work that is expected of her. For those who cannot yet read, provide picture cues and/or demonstrate what is expected. You need to have a lot of visual cues in your classroom.

When you start a discussion of a new topic, give your student a cue about the subject matter—for example, "I'm going to talk about animals." This is particularly important for your speech readers, since only about 40 percent of English can be lip-read.

Know that just because your student is deaf or has a partial hearing loss, she is not necessarily a visual learner. She may, for example, be able to remember best what she is able to hear. Or, she may remember best when she uses tangible objects to learn facts and concepts, as in mathematics. Speak with the special education team and watch your student for clues about how she learns best.

A buddy system may be beneficial for your student. Be sure she wants to participate and be sure everyone else in the classroom has a buddy. It may be a good way to help your student understand directions and instructions. It may also help with social issues, since buddies get to know each other better as they work together on common goals. It's good to change buddies every week so that isolated and separate groups don't get established. You may also want to consider forming buddy teams. Three or four kids to a team is generally a good size. For kids who can read and write independently, one helpful thing that a buddy can volunteer to do for your student is take notes using carbon paper.

Cochlear Implants

A cochlear implant is a device surgically implanted inside the cochlea, a part of the inner ear. This device translates sounds into electrical signals, which are transmitted to the auditory nerve and then to the brain. This surgery is appropriate for some people and not for others and is effective to varying degrees.

If you have a student with a cochlear implant, you should find out if your student has any physical restrictions, such as not using the swings or any gym equipment.

Many people who are deaf do not approve of this surgery. They believe that the deaf culture is a unique and valuable culture that should be cherished. They feel that surgical intervention interferes with a person's sense of belonging in this culture.

Expectations

You should expect your student with a hearing loss to work up to her potential. She needs to work hard for her grades, just like the other kids. Then, she will truly be proud of her accomplishments.

Social Relationships With Peers

You can ask your students and her parents if they or someone else wants to come to your classroom to speak with the other students about hearing loss. Talking about the issue can increase the students' knowledge and make them more empathetic. They can better understand what their peer with hearing loss needs from them. Then, the focus can be on the person and not on the hearing loss.

A Short Interview With a Person Who Has a Hearing Loss

How would you describe your hearing loss?

"I'm legally hard of hearing, mild to moderate. I hear vowels, but I don't hear all the consonants, like *p* and *b*. They don't require as much volume, so I can hear *op-orn* or something like that for *popcorn*. I use context, like if somebody's talking about a snack, I figure it out."

Does your hearing aid help you?

"Yes, a lot. But a hearing aid, it's a little microphone. It magnifies the sound. The difference between a mic and my ear is that a mic is a lot more sensitive. I can hear some sounds, but soft sounds I have trouble with, so my audiologist tried to up the volume to where I would hear the soft sounds, but then that made everything louder.

"You get some distortion with amplification. Like if you've ever been in a place where someone steps up to a mic and it's not exactly right, it sounds tinny, and then you can have a whistling, high sound.

"I control my hearing aid manually. I'm learning how to turn up the volume sometimes, and then to turn it down other times. But it's hard. I've had to learn how to do it."

Low Vision and Blindness

Helen's dad took long-term consulting jobs, so his family moved almost every year. Changing schools was particularly challenging for Helen, because she had albinism, a condition that not only gave her white hair and milky white skin, but also eyes with little pigment. She needed to wear tinted glasses all the time because her eyes were extremely sensitive to light. Her visual acuity was also impaired by this condition.

Fortunately, Helen was not overwhelmed by her physical differences. When she met her new sixth-grade teacher, John O'Rordan, she asked if her mom could come and talk to the other kids about her condition.

"The kids don't make fun of me if my mom comes in," she said.

"That's fine with me," John said. "I know that you're going to be working with Ms. Williams on your reading, and I know that you need to sit away from the window, away from glare. Is there anything else you need?"

"Just treat me like the other kids," Helen said. "That's what my grandma says. She has white hair, too, but she's had it since she was born, just like me. My grandma says that everybody has something to put up with in life. If it's not one darn thing, it's another. My grandma says I'm a regular kid. Treat me like a regular kid."

What is low vision and blindness?

Distance visual acuity is measured in numbers like 20/30. This number means that in the eye being tested, the person can see at 20 feet what a person with average vision can see at 30 feet. He has to stand ten feet closer in order to have comparable vision.

When a person's acuity is measured at 20/70 or less with corrective lenses in the better eye, he is considered to have low vision. When a person's acuity is measured at 20/200 or less with corrective lenses in the better eye, he is considered to be legally blind. A person with a visual field of no greater than 20 degrees may also be considered legally blind (Torres and Corn, 1990).

What are some unique characteristics of students who have low vision or who are blind?

There is no correlation between low vision and blindness and intelligence. These kids are as smart as everybody else. They may, however, experience delays in learning if they are primarily visual learners. Just because students have visual impairments, it does not mean that they are auditory learners. Some students learn best through their visual modalities, using whatever vision they have.

Many factors can influence how vision influences learning in the classroom. For example, Michael, a sixth grader, has low vision measured at 20/90 in his left eye and 20/120 in his right eye. As a little boy, he loved music and sounds, and his parents encouraged his interest by making recorded music available to him. They provided lessons on the clarinet when he asked for them in third grade. Michael consciously developed his auditory sense by paying close attention to sounds. Now he relies on his auditory sense to compensate for his low vision.

Michael's friend Jamana, however, who has a similar level of visual impairment, never focused on using her auditory sense. She loves to touch and feel and look at graphic designs. Her grandmother makes beautiful quilts that Jamana enjoys. In class, Jamana uses the vision she has to learn. Noting individual differences is extremely important.

In addition to difficulty with acuity and the amount of visual field available to them, students may have other types of visual problems. These can include blind spots, or a higher than normal or lower than normal sensitivity to light. Kids may have trouble with peripheral vision and may not be able to see colors or contrasting values.

Some vision conditions fluctuate in their severity. Lighting may influence even normally stable conditions. Surprisingly, the students' emotions or levels of fatigue may also affect them.

What does my student who has low vision or who is blind need from me?

A student diagnosed as having low vision or blindness is eligible to receive services from a special education teacher in your school and/or an itinerant teacher who is called a visual impairment teacher. An orientation and mobility (O&M) instructor can teach your student concepts of spatial awareness and help him learn to move safely through his physical environment. If you are confused about some aspect of your student's program, ask for help from one or more of these professionals.

Setting Up the Classroom

Place your student in the front of the room near the chalkboard and where he can easily hear you. Be aware of glare issues that may cause physical discomfort, especially for students who have excessive sensitivity to light. Discuss the issue of seating with your student, as he knows what type of lighting and seating arrangement will be best for him. Remain flexible. Your student will need to look at books, at the board, at charts, at demonstrations, at people talking to him. Ask yourself questions like, "Is this the best place for him to be during this activity? If I just ask all the kids to come up closer to the chart, will that help not only him but also all of them?" When you are talking or demonstrating, try not to stand in front of a window, especially a sunny window. The glare will cause eye fatigue for everyone.

It's natural to worry about how your student will move around safely in your classroom. Even with careful planning, there can be hazards, such as cabinet doors left ajar by accident, or objects left on the floor that can lead to falls. Support teachers such as the special education teacher, itinerant teacher, or the O&M instructor will work with all your students to create a safe classroom environment. It's normal to worry, and this worry may be good if it keeps everyone alert to any dangers. Your student with a visual impairment needs to gain the confidence to move about independently in the world, so you need to allow him chances to do so in the classroom. Encourage him to move around the room to get supplies and travel to various learning centers. Keeping him at his desk will reinforce feelings of helplessness. The O&M instructor may look at your specific classroom and at all the specific physical issues to find the best way to organize the room.

Moving Around the School

If your student has a severe visual impairment or is blind, the support teacher will show him how to move around the school and how to travel safely to and from your classroom. Occasionally, your student may need a sighted guide—on a field trip to an unfamiliar place, for example. Your student should hold the guide's arm a little above the elbow, and the guide should give verbal cues when necessary, like when the floor level is changing, as with a curb. Here again, your support teacher will teach your student and you the specifics of keeping your student moving and safe.

For fire drills, create a plan of exit from not only your classroom but also from other areas as well, such as the bathroom. You don't want him to panic. The best way to prevent this is to practice exit routes that are designed by an expert in this area.

Also be aware of the special mobility concerns that physical education, the auditorium, lunch, and recess may create. Here again, ask for expert advice from the O&M instructor.

Braille

Braille is a writing system for the blind that uses different combinations of six raised points. Louis Braille (1809–1852) who became blind when he was three years old, created the system.

Talking With Your Student

When you approach a student who is blind, always say your name, and teach your other students to do the same. It takes a lot of energy for your student to move safely around your classroom and to focus on his learning. He does not need the added burden of trying to figure out who is coming close and who wants to interact with him.

Be aware of how you praise your student. Good teachers often smile and use body language to express approval and delight. Your student with a visual impairment may not see these signs of approval, however, so it is important to remember to provide verbal praise for him also. Develop the habit of accompanying your smile with comments like "That makes me happy when you do such good work," and "I'm giving you a thumbs up."

Don't be concerned about using phrases such as "I can't see what you're talking about," or "Oh, now I see." There are so many common references to vision in everyday language that trying to screen them out will make you sound unnatural. Kids with visual impairment are used to such references and most will not be offended. If you have a student whom you suspect is offended, speak with him about this.

Understanding Your Student

Some students with visual impairments feel uncomfortable when attention is drawn to their limited vision. They may resist asking for help and may not want to use special devices. It's natural for kids to want to be just like everyone else. Sometimes, however, your student may need the extra help, and you have to judge when this is more important than his preference to do things on his own.

Some kids actively hide their visual impairment. Pay close attention and intervene when you see this happening. Ira Fingold's fourth-grade student Leo, for example, is normally an active and happy member of his fourth-grade class. His reading group had just finished the novel *Sarah, Plain and Tall* by Patricia MacLachlan and was seated at a round table creating an alternative book report. The group had decided to make a new and improved book jacket for a paperback version of the book, and the other three kids were happily discussing what the front cover should look like. Leo, however, was turned away from the group, looking out the window. Ira suspected that he was feeling uncomfortable because he didn't want the other kids to know that he is color-blind, in addition to his other visual issues. Ira took a deep breath and went back to his desk to figure out what to do. He absently picked up two paperback books on his desk and looked at the jackets. The front covers were beautiful; then he turned to the back. Aha—both books had reviews on the back covers. Leo enjoys writing. He has excellent critical thinking skills. Ira went over to the group and said, "You know, don't forget about the back cover. See these books? They have reviews back there. Do one or more of you want to write a couple of reviews?" Leo nodded his head. "Oh, good. I'm sure you'll do a great job."

Curriculum

Use a lot of verbal cues in your instruction. While you do this, be aware that if your student has a serious impairment, he may need help understanding concepts, like "below" and "around," that are visually based. Teach your student to give you a signal if he is confused.

If you are writing on the chalkboard or on an easel with a large pad of paper, make sure the visual information is accessible to your student. If the activity is more interactive, say out loud what you are writing.

Talk with the special education teacher about the size of print that your student needs to function independently. Also, there are special papers available for him to write on. Some of these have wide, bold lines. Others have raised lines.

Some students with significant visual impairments have trouble producing handwriting and, once they have produced it, being able to see and understand it. Keyboarding skills can be extremely helpful for these students. Bob King's sixth-grade student Alex is learning proper keyboarding skills. Before, he hunted for the letters, but now one of his IEP goals is "Alex will be able to use proper fingers for touch-typing the alphabet." Bob makes sure that Alex practices this skill for at least fifteen minutes every day in the classroom.

Expectations

If he has no other learning issues, your student should be expected to do the same work as the other kids. He may, however, need more time to complete certain tasks if his impaired vision slows him down. For example, if all the kids are working on a report on an animal and your student Thomas has chosen the black bear, he may need some help accessing the print in the resource books, since the ones in your classroom are not all available in large print. He may need to use a magnifying system or ask someone to read to him. Thomas may not be able to produce as much material as his classmates in the same amount of time because of the cumbersome nature of this task.

Tests and Homework

It is generally considered appropriate on tests to allow your student to have time and a half if his visual impairment is slowing him down. If your student is blind, the visual-impairment teacher may sometimes arrange for a person to transcribe the test into Braille and then to translate your student's responses back into written form. Students who are blind may take tests orally or use a tape recorder or computer. Since it is important for your student to practice working with text or Braille, it's best to avoid relying on oral tests.

For homework, use the general rule that your student should have to spend as much time as everyone else, not more. This is not always easy to judge, and you can consult with your student and his parents about it.

Impaired Vision Aids

There are many different devices that help people with impaired vision.

- ◌ Computers with extra large monitors can display large print. There are even special printers that print in Braille.

- ◌ CCTVs (closed-circuit televisions) project greatly enlarged print and other material onto a TV screen. They can project in black and white and color and can vary the level of contrast and illumination.

- ◌ Handheld magnifiers increase the image close at hand. Little telescopes help your student see more distant images.

- ◌ Large-print books

- ◌ Talking calculators "speak" the numbers that are entered and then give the final answer. The abacus, a frame with movable counting pieces, is also useful for some students.

In addition to these devices, these two organizations offer recorded books:

Library of Congress National Library Service for the Blind and Physically Handicapped (Talking Book Program; 202-707-5100 or 800-424-8567)

Recording for the Blind and Dyslexic (609-452-0606 or 800-221-4792); www.rfbd.org

Social Relationships With Peers

Be aware of your student's social functioning, especially during unstructured times like lunch and recess. If your student is new to your school or for some other reason the other kids don't know him, they may interpret his behavior as withdrawn or even stuck-up. He may simply be having trouble seeing his peers or reading facial expressions. This may make him reluctant to introduce himself or reach out in other ways. He may need a class buddy to help him with this.

Sometimes it helps for a parent or a specialist to speak with your class about vision impairment. This can be a general talk and does not have to be focused on the particular issues and needs of your student, especially if he is sensitive about this. Sometimes kids with visual impairments feel more comfortable when they know that their peers understand their condition.

Elena's Story

When she was a little girl, Elena had a brain tumor. It was operated on successfully, but the doctors told her and her family that because of the operation, she would gradually lose her sight and would eventually become completely blind. Elena could see that her family was horribly upset.

Time passed and things settled into a normal routine. Elena did begin to lose her sight, but she hid that fact from her family and her teachers. Because the vision loss was gradual, she learned to compensate at every stage. No one knew that her vision loss had begun and that it was, in fact, quite advanced.

Around seventh grade, Elena became blind. Still, she hid it. She always asked a brother or sister to go with her to the store, to school, or anywhere. She'd casually stand near them as she walked and would occasionally touch their arm or take their hand. If she needed to get milk for her mom, she'd ask her little brother to pick the gallon that he liked best from the cooler. In school, she asked other students to hand her things, and they were happy to oblige. Elena finally told her family about her blindness. She doesn't remember exactly why she told them, or when.

Elena's deception was helped by her warm and outgoing personality. People in her family and in her classrooms just expected to help and support Elena. They got used to her ways. You will probably not encounter such a dramatic example, but be aware of the possibility.

Speech and Language Disorders

Charlie never spoke in class and seemed withdrawn and isolated from his kindergarten classmates. At the beginning of the year, Suzanne O'Reilly thought he was just painfully shy, but as she watched Charlie more closely, she began to notice some unusual things. Charlie seemed to understand what was said to him. But when he tried to speak, he searched for his words, often pausing for long periods of time and even physically squirming. Charlie answered in short phrases of one or two words, and he often added the nonsense word "tam."

One afternoon, Suzanne asked him what activity he'd like to do at the science center.

"Tam . . . I want . . . I . . . tam. . . ." Charlie said. Charlie dropped the book he was holding and walked to the far end of the room.

"He talks like a baby," a classmate said.

Just by chance, Suzanne got a phone call from Charlie's mom later that afternoon.

"I'm worried about Charlie's speech," his mom said. "We used to think he'd grow out of it, but . . . what do you think?"

"I think he should be tested. There may be something we can do to help."

Charlie's evaluation determined that he had developmental apraxia, a condition in which the child knows what he wants to say but has trouble producing the right sounds and words in the proper sequence. Once a diagnosis was made, Charlie received treatment from a speech-language pathologist.

What is a speech and language disorder?

A speech and language disorder affects a person's ability to communicate. It may affect one or more of the following areas:

❋ Receptive language: the ability to discriminate speech sounds and to understand and process spoken language efficiently

❋ Expressive language: the ability to express thoughts and feelings with spoken language

* Articulation: the ability to consistently, accurately, and fluently produce speech sounds
* Voice: the ability to produce spoken language with good tone and pitch

More information about speech and language disorders can be obtained from the American Speech-Language-Hearing Association.

What are some unique characteristics of students with speech and language disorders?

Speech and language disorders may affect all communications, including the clarity, accuracy, and freedom of personal conversations, as well as the ability to read social cues. This can greatly impact social relationships.

Speech and language disorders may affect all aspects of academic learning, and students with these issues often perform below their potential in school. For most people, the abilities to listen and speak develop first, and these are the bases for reading, writing, and spelling. Written language skills then inform oral language, as when new vocabulary is learned through reading. Oral and written language instruct each other, so a speech and/or language problem interrupts this flow.

Concept development is also affected, since children learn to structure much of the world through language. Students with these issues may have difficulty using language to problem solve and to think creatively and logically.

There are four basic types of speech and language disorders: receptive, expressive, articulation, and voice.

Receptive Language Disorders

People with this type of disorder have difficulty deciphering the sounds they are hearing. A woman named Claire reports that when she was in elementary school, her speech was inaccurate, and she couldn't read or spell. Her teachers felt that it must be a hearing problem, so they kept referring her for hearing testing—and Claire kept passing. Now an adult, Claire has been properly diagnosed as having a difficulty with auditory discrimination. She can hear the sounds of the language, but many of them, especially the short vowels, seem the same to her.

A second skill people need for efficient receptive language is the ability to organize and understand the meaning of what is spoken to them. This is called central auditory processing. These listening skills are extremely important and affect the ability to follow directions. Frank Pezzalla's fourth-grade student Roland was sitting at his desk when Frank said to the class,

"Please take out your science notebooks and get your pencils, and then, don't go to the science table, but go to the back of the room because we have a special experiment set up there." Roland got out his notebook and went right to the science table. He was proud that he got there first. Roland understood about the notebook, but then missed the next direction. In his effort to understand, he focused on the words *science table* and thought his teacher wanted him to go there.

Expressive Language Disorders

All of us have word banks in our heads in which we deposit words and phrases. Once a word is learned, it is put into long-term storage where it is available for the next appropriate use. Unfortunately, people with expressive language issues have difficulty retrieving these words. They know what they want to say, but they can't think of the exact word. To cope, they often pause, or repeat the preceding phrase, or add verbal fillers, such as "umm" or "well." They often substitute words with less precise meaning, such as "stuff" for "clothes." This condition, often called aphasia, causes spoken language to be stilted, dysfluent, and uncomfortable for both the speaker and the listener.

Articulation Disorders

Mispronunciations are common at different developmental stages. It is only at about 6 ½ years of age, for example, that typical children can consistently produce the *sh*, *th*, and *r* sounds. In addition, physical issues, such as recurring ear infections, especially before age three, may delay the attainment of proper pronunciation. Mispronunciations are considered problematic only when they stubbornly persist. Mispronunciations can be distortions ("bulack" for *black*), substitutions (*pet* for *bet*), or omissions (*at* for *bat*).

Other types of mispronunciations are lisps and stuttering. A lisp involves not easily distinguishing the *sh*, *th*, and *s* sounds. Stuttering is either an inability to produce a sound or the repetition of a sound. People who stutter characteristically repeat parts of words, or substitute "uh" for a vowel, or use a broken rhythm. At this time, the exact cause of stuttering is unknown.

Two other articulation conditions that are known to be organically based, however, are dysarthria (weakness in some muscles of the face) and oral apraxia (difficulty coordinating the muscles of the face).

Voice Disorders

Some students have speech that is either too soft or too loud. The quality of the voice can also be problematic. These issues make it difficult for others to understand what they are saying.

What does my student with a speech and/or language disorder need from me?

Understanding Your Student

Take the time to talk with your student's speech and language pathologist to find out what social and academic areas are being affected by her issues. Is her difficulty with receptive language making reading (and especially reading comprehension) really hard for her? Is her inability to discriminate between speech sounds making spelling almost impossible? Is she having trouble expressing her thoughts, and is this making participating in group discussions in science and social studies problematic? Your awareness is an important first step.

If your student with a speech and language disorder is bilingual or multilingual, speak with her speech and language pathologist to learn how this might affect her language functioning in your classroom.

Talking With Your Student

When giving directions or providing important instruction, be aware of the pace and tone of your speech. Speak clearly, concisely, and directly. For example, avoid going off on a tangent, telling side stories, or giving additional examples. Using organizing words, such as *first*, *next*, and *last* also helps.

As much as possible, seat your student away from auditory and visual distractions so she can focus on listening to the language she is receiving. It is a good idea, in fact, to actually teach your student how to pay attention. Start with physical factors. Through role playing and/or modeling, teach her how to sit quietly and watch the speaker. A third grader named Helena found that she could do this best if she clasped her hands on her lap. Judy, a fifth grader, likes to hold a pencil. Find out what works. Teach your student to focus on only one speaker at a time and to try to concentrate as much as possible on the meaning of what is being said. To help your student practice, always make sure that you have her attention when you are speaking to her. If you are asking your student to listen, do not expect her to do anything else at the same time, such as taking notes.

If your student has a receptive language disorder, notice how many directions she can understand at one time. For example, a second-grade student, Matilda, gazes up with a confused expression when asked to take her spelling book out of her desk and open it to a certain page. This is a two-step direction. Perhaps Matilda needs a pause after she's asked to take out her spelling book (one direction). Then, once her book is on her desk, she can hear and understand that she should open it to a particular page (one direction). Watch your student carefully so that you can successfully give directions to her.

Give a student with any type of expressive language disorder plenty of time to speak, and don't allow other students to interrupt or "help" by providing a word. The student shouldn't be hurried. Your job is to make sure she gets the time she needs to find the verbal material in her memory bank. You are the guardian of this quiet time.

Curriculum

Provide concrete and visual examples of concepts that you are presenting. Talking and/or writing are not enough. If you are teaching a unit on multiplication, for example, have sets of items, like beans or blocks, that your student can see, touch, and move. This will reinforce the verbal discussion.

Adding meaning to unfamiliar verbal material, like new vocabulary, may greatly help your student with a receptive language disorder retain the new words. For this reason, third-grade teacher Louise Farrell adds other elements of instruction to her simple definitions of new words for her student Laura. Laura has an IEP goal that states, "Laura will learn new vocabulary that occurs naturally in content teaching in the classroom." Louise asks Laura to talk about the new word, and to use it in a sentence. If the new word is a verb, she asks her to pantomime it. Louise talks about opposites of the word and lists similar words. She places the new word in a cluster of meaning.

If your student has an expressive language issue, speak with her speech and language pathologist to decide how to handle oral discussions or oral reports in class. Should your student be challenged to do some public speaking, or would that be a humiliating and destructive experience? Should alternatives that will have a positive impact be created?

Social Relationships

Deal directly with teasing. Kids with expressive language issues can be very vulnerable to both overt and subtle forms of teasing, such as mimicking. Speak directly to all students involved. Explain the issues so that the teasers will understand, but also be very clear that no teasing of any type will be tolerated.

Stuttering

Stuttering is a unique problem that can be very destructive in terms of social relationships. Kids may get nervous about their stuttering, and this often makes the stuttering worse. To help a student who stutters, give her plenty of time to say what she wants to communicate. Don't finish her sentences for her or give her any words. Stay calm and quiet, and maintain eye contact. As much as possible, let her know that you are listening to *what* she is saying, not *how* she is saying it and that you know that she has valuable information to give you. It is interesting to note that stuttering tends to increase when people are talking on the telephone, and decrease during oral reading, whispering, and singing.

It may help a student who stutters to know that she is not alone. One good way to do this is to tell her about famous people who have had this difficulty. For example, King Charles I of England stuttered, as did Isaac Newton, the scientist who discovered the law of gravity. The actress Marilyn Monroe sometimes stuttered. Your student may be very impressed to know that James Earl Jones, who provided the voice for Darth Vader in the *Star Wars* movies, has struggled with stuttering.

Cause of Stuttering

There is increasing evidence indicating that stuttering is not caused by trauma or other emotional issues, but rather by a neurological problem.

Physical Disabilities and Health Impairments

One minute during recess, Tara was quietly standing next to her friend Anna, and the next, she was on the ground, her arms and legs jerking uncontrollably. The seizure lasted only half a minute, but when Tara regained consciousness, she felt exhausted . . . and humiliated. All of the fifth graders were out at recess. All of the kids could have seen her.

Anna was bending over her. "I'll get Ms. Griffin."

"No. I'll be all right."

"You know you have to sleep after one of these," Anna said.

"I don't care. Just leave me alone. Leave me alone."

Anna sat down next to her. "Nobody saw," she said. "All the kids were watching the softball game."

Silence.

"I mean, look. Nobody's coming anywhere near us."

"They think they'll catch it," Tara said.

"They know they won't catch it," Anna said. "Look, the lilac bush blocked the view. Nobody saw."

Tara looked up then. "You really think so?"

"Yeah." Anna took Tara's hand and helped her up. "Let's go and get Ms. Griffin. "Maybe you can take a nap in the nurse's office."

What is a physical disability and what is a health impairment?

In the world of special education, a physical disability is a physical impairment that is so severe it affects a student's educational performance. The impairment may be skeletal, muscular, or neurological. It may be caused by a congenital anomaly, disease, or other factor such as an accident. Three of the most common impairments in students are cerebral palsy (a neurological condition), spina bifida (a neurological condition), and muscular dystrophy (a musculoskeletal condition).

A health impairment is an acute or chronic health problem such as a heart condition, lead poisoning, or diabetes that may affect a student's available energy and alertness for learning.

More information about specific physical disabilities and health impairments can be obtained from national organizations. The National Health Information Center (NHIC; 800-336-4797) provides referrals to appropriate organizations.

What are some unique characteristics of students with physical disabilities or health impairments?

There are many types of physical disabilities and health impairments that vary widely in terms of levels of severity. In addition, each student's emotional reaction to physical challenges is highly individual. Every person with a physical or health impairment is unique and needs to be seen as such.

The physical disability or health impairment may cause emotional distress. Some of your students may have experienced trauma because of an accident or illness. Extended hospitalizations or treatments may also cause stress in students' lives. Some students may see themselves as different from the other kids, causing social difficulties as well.

What does my student with a physical disability or physical impairment need from me?

Understanding Your Student

It is very important for you to know about the particular physical disability or health impairment your student faces. Contact information for organizations that can provide you with information is found on page 128.

Your student lives not only with his physical disability or health issue, but also with the emotional impact of it. He may be discouraged at times or under a lot of stress because of a certain medical treatment he is undergoing. It is important to watch him and to provide support and encouragement on those days when he seems upset or sad. If your student remains upset for a long period of time, report this to the special education team.

Your student may need to be away from class for medical appointments, or for more extended periods of time for other medical purposes. Treat this as a normal part of his school program. This is a portion of what your student needs. The more you help to normalize his time away, the less upset your student will be about it.

Many physical issues present unique challenges. For example, Thomas Sanchez's seventh-grade student Peter suddenly became very agitated during a discussion of the Civil War in history class. Peter had been contributing interesting insights to the discussion. Suddenly he was turning his head from side to side and not paying attention. Peter is confined to a wheelchair because of muscular dystrophy and has limited use of his arms. When Mr. Sanchez approached Peter, he realized that a bee had entered the classroom and was circling Peter. Because Peter's mobility was limited, he felt frightened. Mr. Sanchez did exactly the right thing. He assumed that Peter's sudden change in behavior was being caused by an unknown factor and went to investigate. As soon as he discovered the cause, he removed the bee and then helped Peter get back to history class. Every physical challenge can make students afraid of widely diverse things. Become aware of your student's particular fears so that you can help alleviate them and take quick action when an unavoidable situation arises.

The Classroom Environment

Be aware of any accommodations listed on your student's IEP. Accommodations may affect homework policy, seating arrangement in the classroom, the use of readers or taped books, and attendance policies. It's a good idea to read your student's IEP first to get an overview of goals and objectives and accommodations, and then to study it more carefully for its implications in your student's daily life in your classroom.

If your student has mobility issues, be aware of any physical barrier that can cause problems. Is there an extra little half-step in your school building that could cause a student who has limited balance to fall?

Fire Drills

Fire drills may pose particular difficulty for students with mobility issues. The special education team should have an exit plan for your student, and you need to be aware of it. For example, Mary Lokensgard's fifth-grade student Charlie is in a wheelchair because of a serious car accident. Mary needs to know what to do if there is a fire drill (or a fire) when her class is visiting the library on the second floor. Charlie can't use the elevator, and Mary does not have the physical strength to carry him. The special education team arranged for two teachers who do have this physical strength to first check the library for Charlie and carry him down the stairs if necessary. Mary needs to know which teachers have agreed to do this, and if they don't arrive immediately at the library, she needs to find them, if possible.

Expectations

Your student needs to be treated like everyone else. He may need certain physical modifications to the environment, special foods, or certain adaptive devices. Some days, he may not have as much physical energy as on other days. It is important, however, that you expect him to work up to his potential, whatever that potential is on any given day. The physical issue should never become an excuse for limited effort. Also, expect your student to follow the same rules of behavior as the other kids. Doing so will help him become a valued member of your class.

Don't let your student's physical challenge be his primary label. Helen Adamson's first-grade student Adam was born with shortened arms. His family has always been highly supportive of him, and Helen knows that he's growing up in an atmosphere of love and acceptance. When Adam entered her classroom, she sensed that he expected to be treated just like every other child, and this turned out to be true. When other people ask her about Adam, Helen describes him as a bright little boy who already has attained beginning reading skills, and he has shortened arms. She does not first describe him only as a boy with shortened arms. The way you talk about a student is important because it can affect the way you and other people think about him. You want your focus to be on him as a person, not as a child with impairments.

Social Relationships With Peers

It may be helpful to speak with the other children about your student's physical disability or health impairment. This needs to be decided on a case-by-case basis and, before you do this, always check with your student and with your student's parents to make sure this is what they wish to happen. A parent or an expert can come to speak to your class. This not only provides other students with information, but it may also lessen fears that other students have.

Emotional Disturbances and/ or Behavioral Disorders

Victor had spent a lot of time in the courts in the past two years as his mom and dad fought for custody of him. Sometimes, he lived in Ohio with his mom, and then he was back in Rhode Island with his dad. And then there was the day his mom picked him up for a weeklong visit and just kept driving south . . . and settled in Florida. A detective his dad hired found him six months later.

Now, Victor was 8, and it looked like the custody battles were finally over. Victor was living with his dad and was back at his old school. But the bubbly, happy child that people had seen in kindergarten and first grade now appeared frightened and withdrawn.

Victor received an evaluation and was seeing the school counselor every Wednesday afternoon. One day, he refused to go.

"Don't you like Ms. Williams?" Ray Hellerman, his teacher, asked.

"The kids make fun of me. They say I'm crazy just like my mom."

"Hmm, not good. Is it okay with you if I tell Ms. Williams what you just told me?"

"Okay," Victor said.

Ms. Williams stopped seeing Victor by himself. Instead, she came into the classroom for a few weeks and helped lots of kids with their writing during writing time. When she finally asked Victor and two other boys to come to her office to play a math game, they readily agreed.

Now, three months later, other kids sometimes ask to join him as Victor quietly gets out of his seat and goes to meet Ms. Williams. Sometimes Victor asks his teacher if they can come. Other times, he says he'd like to go alone.

What are emotional disturbances and/or behavioral disorders?

Emotional disturbances and behavioral disorders can look very different from one another in the classroom. One child may be extremely withdrawn; another may be oppositional and aggressive. Emotional disturbances and behavioral disorders are linked together because current understanding indicates that both are based in difficulties feeling comfortable with oneself and others. They may have the following commonalities:

* A difficulty with learning
* A difficulty establishing and maintaining successful relationships with classmates and teachers
* Inexplicable reactions or feelings triggered by seemingly normal circumstances
* General unhappiness and/or depression
* The tendency to develop fears or physical symptoms

These difficulties appear over a long period of time, develop to a significant degree, and are not caused by intellectual, sensory, or other health issues (Adapted from IDEA).

What are some unique characteristics of students with emotional disturbances and/or behavioral disorders?

These children may have experienced difficult family situations, trauma outside the home, or harsh circumstances such as poverty and/or homelessness. However, they come from all walks of life, and the cause of their distress is not always observable. In addition, some of the challenges once regarded as purely emotional are now believed to be partially, if not completely, organic in cause. We still have a lot to learn about emotional disturbances and behavioral disorders. They are extremely complex and diverse.

There are, however, common conditions that have been identified. Anxiety can be a major factor in some students' lives. All of us are anxious at times, but if this increased state of vigilance and apprehension becomes habitual, students can feel threatened by almost any situation. Sadness is another normal feeling that, for some students, becomes persistent and severe, sometimes developing into depression.

Students who have emotional and/or behavioral disorders often have difficulty controlling their impulses. If they want to throw their books on the floor, they do so. If they want to yell at a peer, they do. They also have trouble handling frustration. All students face irritations and problems during the school day, but students with emotional and/or behavioral disorders can't just "get over it" easily. They tend to get upset, and the unhappy and unsettled feelings linger and affect the rest of their day. If a student tends to act out her feelings, this can become aggression against herself or others. If she tends to withdraw, she can become more isolated and alone.

There are many types of emotional and behavioral distress. The following are some common ones:

* ✷ Phobia: an uncontrollable fear, such as a fear of heights or spiders, or even of school.

* ✷ Anorexia: an unwillingness to eat, which can lead to self-starvation.

* ✷ Bulimia: eating too much and then immediately throwing up.

* ✷ Bipolar disorder: a disorder in which there are severe mood swings between excitement and depression.

* ✷ Character disorder: a disorder in which there is little guilt or remorse shown following aggressive or hurtful behavior.

* ✷ Oppositional disorder: a resistance to obeying school rules and following teacher directions.

* ✷ Conduct disorder: This can take many forms, such as aggressive behavior toward people and/or property. It can include lying, stealing, and setting fires.

* ✷ Obsessive-compulsive disorder: repetitive thoughts causing great anxiety, which then compel a person to perform actions to extricate him- or herself from the obsessive thoughts. Now usually considered neurologically based, it may also be induced by severe and persistent trauma.

What does my student with an emotional disturbance and/or behavioral disorder need from me?

Expectations

You need to establish clear and consistent expectations for behavior. The specificity of the rules may vary depending on grade level. It is appropriate in a kindergarten class, for example, to say, "We raise our hands when we want to speak in class." For a sixth-grade class, rules can be more general, such as, "We treat each other with respect," and "We will never interfere with another person's learning." Creating the right rules and expectations is important. Often, it is most effective to create and discuss these rules with your entire class.

Dealing With Behavior

If your student has a conduct disorder and is aggressive either verbally or physically toward peers, this is a serious situation that should be dealt with directly. Make it clear that no aggression, either verbal or physical, will be tolerated in your classroom and that the consequences for this behavior will be consistently applied. Be aware that sometimes other students may bait or try to create problems for the student who has a conduct disorder. This is an unfortunate situation that needs to be dealt with as an act of aggression. If you are alert and respond quickly, you can significantly reduce the problem.

It is often helpful to have a time-out space in the classroom. This can be something as simple as a desk or a chair that is positioned behind a screen. The area should be uncluttered, providing as little external stimulation as possible. Your student may choose to go there if she is feeling overwhelmed, or you can ask her to go there if you feel she's behaving inappropriately. The time-out area should be portrayed as a place of sanctuary and help, rather than as a place of punishment and dismissal. Make it clear to your student that you want her to be able to rejoin her classmates as soon as possible.

For a student to be successful in your classroom, she needs to respond to verbal directions, such as, "Please go to the time-out area until I ask you to come back to your desk." If she is not able to follow your verbal directions, you need to tell the special education team about this and ask for further help from them.

Have clear and absolutely consistent consequences for negative behavior. If you are unclear about what consequences are appropriate for your student, ask the special education team for help.

If you have a student who has symptoms of obsessive-compulsive disorder, you may need to be creative to help her succeed in your classroom. The first step is to observe if she is exhibiting any compulsions that are destructive. Karen Pellens's fifth-grade student Jesse, for example, needs to have her name and date placed on her paper in the exact same place on every page on which she writes. She will check and recheck and then will erase and try over and over to get it exactly as she wants it. This takes a lot of time away from Jesse's learning. One solution Karen found was to provide Jesse with papers where her name was already printed. (Karen created these on a copy machine). Light lines were added where Jesse needed to place numbers to represent the date. By strategizing with your student, you can often come up with practical and significant ways to make her compulsions less obvious, less time-consuming, and less destructive.

Talking With Your Student

If your student has an oppositional disorder, it is important to learn how to speak with her when her disorder is triggered. She will want to argue with you, to talk and talk. She will use lots of verbalization to counter any reasonable expectation you have or any reasonable explanation you make. And she won't do what you want her to do. Mary Wong had a fifth-grade student named Julie who was challenging. Julie was supposed to begin work on her report on the state of Florida. She decided that she wanted to read her silent-reading book instead. She told her teacher, "This report is stupid. I want to read my book, and my mother says that it's good for me to read, and that's what I'm going to do." Mary replied, "Julie, you have a choice. You can write about an animal in Florida, or you can write about a special flower." Julie said, "It's too noisy in here, and I don't want to write about Florida, and I want to work on the computer. It's stupid to write about a state. I don't learn anything from that. I learn a lot more from reading." Mary responded, "Julie, you have a choice. You can write about an animal in Florida, or you can write about a special flower." This conversation may go on for a while, but Mary needs to continue saying the same simple thing in a calm, even voice.

Mary chose this particular "mantra" because Julie originally chose Florida for her state report. Julie loves animals and flowers. Mary recognized that Julie was probably feeling overwhelmed and that she needed help to be able to come back and participate in the class activity. Julie didn't *want* it, but she *needed* for Mary to be in control of the situation.

If Julie continued to refuse to work on her report after several more repetitions of the mantra, one thing Mary could do is to ask her to go to a time-out area, where interactions with others and outside stimulation will be at a minimum. She can then tell Julie that she needs to sit there quietly, until she is ready to begin working on her Florida report.

Removing Julie to this quiet space does three things: it gives her a chance to relax, it removes inadvertent reinforcement from the other kids for her oppositional behavior, and it makes her very bored. This boredom will help her revisit her decision not to participate in the class activity. Eventually, writing about an animal or a flower in Florida will start looking pretty good.

Understanding Your Student

Be aware of any extreme reactions to seemingly "normal" situations. For example, one day a visitor came to Henry Balinski's fifth grade to demonstrate how to make a quilt. When the visitor took a small ironing board and iron out of a box, Henry's student Claudio suddenly jumped up from his desk, threw his books on the floor, and ran out of the room. Since a paraprofessional was in the room, it was possible for Henry to follow Claudio to where he was crying on the playground under a tree. Henry sat next to him and told him that he would stay with him until he began to feel better. When Claudio began to relax, Henry asked him if he needed anything.

In Claudio's situation, it is important not to question his behavior. If Claudio wanted to talk to Henry about the incident, he would freely do so. Never pry. If your student has a sudden and inexplicable emotional reaction, you can say things like, "I can see that you are upset. Is there anything I can do to help you?" Offer caring support, and let your student know that you are concerned about him. You can report the incident to the members of the special education team as soon as you have the privacy to do so.

Even though Henry was curious about why Claudio had this reaction, it was most important to focus on taking care of him and reporting the incident to the people who deal with his emotional needs.

Structuring the Day

Kids with emotional and behavior issues need familiarity and comfort. For this reason, it will help your student to have a structured school day, in which lessons occur at regular times and a regular routine is followed for the logistics, such as lining up for lunch. Predictability helps her relax. If there is a need for a change, tell your student ahead of time so that she feels better prepared for it.

Curriculum

Be careful when giving assignments that deal with family matters and living situations, such as asking students to create family trees or write family histories. Your student may have information she does not wish to reveal. Also, she may need to deal with this information in a therapeutic setting, not in a classroom.

Asking your student to interview members of her family may be problematic. Even if you give her a choice of whom to interview, she might not feel comfortable interviewing anyone. This puts her in a stressful situation in which she may feel she needs to keep secrets.

Your student may not understand or accept what has happened or what is happening to her outside of school, and it can be destructive to ask her to write about these things. Always provide a less emotionally charged alternative to an assignment involving family.

Check your student's IEP to see if she has any special needs other than social and emotional ones. When Laura Manning read her new sixth-grade student Andrea's current functioning profile on her IEP, she learned that Andrea has a mild form of dyscalcula. Laura resolved to talk with the special education teacher to find out what services Andrea would receive from the special education team and how Andrea's math program should be modified in her classroom.

Your Responsibility for Your Student's Safety and Well-Being

If one of your students is fleeing abuse and living in an underground shelter with a parent, her physical presence at school needs to be kept secret. For this reason, it is critically important not to take photographs of her or to videotape special programs in which she participates. You should also not talk about her situation with anyone other than the special education team. Keep her safety foremost in your mind.

Be aware of practical aspects of your student's life. Does she seem lethargic by midmorning? If kids bring snacks from home, does she have one? Is her winter coat threadbare or not warm enough? Are her shoes worn out? If you notice things like this, report them to the special education team. There may be ways to help by referring her family to agencies.

Remain aware of your responsibility to report any signs of abuse or neglect that you observe. In some states, such as Massachusetts, teachers are mandated reporters. Check with your special education team about the legal obligations in your state. In general, however, it is very important for you to report to your special education team and your school principal any signs that your student may be being abused or neglected.

We are all too aware of how some children can injure and even kill others. If your student talks to you about the desire to do this, report it immediately to your special education team. Also, if your student talks to you about hurting herself, take this very seriously and report it immediately. A trained person should speak with her. Sometimes we feel that we are overreacting if we report a casual conversation about self-injury. You are never overreacting in a situation like that. Kids don't talk about self-injury unless a part of them is thinking about it. Your report and the subsequent intervention may be preventive. It should tell your student that her teachers have noticed that she is upset and that they are going to help her.

Tomasso's Story

Four-year-old Tomasso took a long trip to spend the summer with his grandparents in Chile. During his stay, his grandfather died. When Tomasso came home after the funeral, he no longer spoke. This formerly chatty little boy stared silently at anyone who tried to converse with him. This behavior continued in kindergarten and first grade.

This rare condition is called selective mutism. Psychologists used to believe that the condition was based solely on trauma or other childhood issues. Now, however, they believe it to be based in the chemistry of the brain. As reported in the *Boston Globe* on April 15, 2003, a psychiatrist named Bruce Black began studying selective mutism in the 1980s. He first read all the theories about what might cause the condition, including emotional trauma or injury to the mouth. Then, he started doing research with 35 children who are selectively mute. He found that 70 percent of these children's families have a history of social phobia, and 37 percent of the children's families have a history of selective mutism. Dr. Black believes that a child who becomes selectively mute has two intense fear centers in the brain that can be triggered by pressure to speak. It is like a severe form of fear of public speaking.

Why did Tomasso become silent after his grandfather died? No one knows for sure. But we can speculate that the death triggered Tomasso's fear centers, and Tomasso then developed the habit of not speaking. It was his way of coping with the intense anxiety that speaking could arouse.

The good news is that there is now real hope for children like Tomasso. As with other psychiatric conditions, medication can help a great deal. Also, a form of therapy called cognitive behavioral therapy can help him learn to re-enter the world of speech.

What Do I Need to Know About the Special Education System ?

Background

How did special education get started?

Special education has its origins in the civil rights movement. Our society began to develop a belief that all people deserved to have equal opportunity and that federal laws could be created to facilitate this.

This belief spread to the educational system. Fred Adamson, a man with severe dyslexia who grew up in the 1950s and 60s, says that when he was in elementary school, his teachers were quite upset when he couldn't learn to read or write. Because he acted up, one of his teachers placed his desk behind hers in the front of the room. By fourth grade, he was spending most of the school day helping the custodian do various chores around the building. Needless to say, he dropped out of school at 16.

Many of Fred's teachers wanted to help him. They just didn't know how, and there were no systems in place to help them become more effective. At that time, there were no laws that demanded that Fred receive a free, appropriate education.

What are the laws that govern special education?

The basic law that established special education was passed by Congress in 1975 and was called Public Law 94-142. This law provided federal funding to school districts for special education. The law was updated in 1997 and is now called the Individuals with Disabilities Education Act (IDEA). It ensures that students with defined and proven disabilities receive a free and appropriate education in the least restrictive environment. This law established that special education is not a place, such as a resource room or a separate school, but instead a carefully designed package of services and instruction for each individual student. These services and instruction can and should be provided for the student in the regular classroom whenever possible. This is the basis for the inclusion model.

There are two other important laws that help people with disabilities. Section 504 of the Rehabilitation Act of 1973 states that no person with a disability can, because of that disability, be denied access to or refused the benefits of a program that receives federal aid because of his disability. Thus, a student in a wheelchair can't be kept away from a library because he can't climb the stairs of the building. He can't be kept out of school because there is no accessible bathroom. In both cases, access has to be created.

The Americans with Disabilities Act of 1990 (ADA) clarifies the definition of a disability and expands the protections first sought by Section 504 of the Rehabilitation Act of 1973. Now, all programs and services, not just those receiving federal aid, must provide equal opportunity for people with disabilities. This includes workplaces, public places such as hotels and restaurants, and transportation. Both of these laws complement IDEA.

Eligibility

How do students become identified as having special needs?

First, someone notices that a student is not happy or is not functioning well in the classroom, or that something is "just not right." That someone may be you. If one of your students is just not actively and happily engaged in learning, note when and where this is happening. It can be very helpful to keep a written log, in which you jot down notes such as, "Anthony kept staring out the widow during science, and when I asked him a question that I was sure he knew, he just stared at me." Taking notes like this over time can show valuable patterns.

If you or someone else, often a parent, expresses concern about a student, the student can be referred for a formal evaluation to determine if disabilities exist.

What happens if I have a student in my class whom I think has special needs, but the student's parents do not wish to explore this?

Parents play a significant role in the special education process, and if they do not wish to engage in this process, nothing can be done. In this case, accept the parents' wishes and continue to calmly report to them what is happening in the classroom. Also, keep careful notes about your concerns. Write these notes in terms of what you observe. For example, "This afternoon [record the date and time] Anna refused to take the class spelling test. She threw the test paper on the floor and started crying at her desk." Don't write about your feelings ("I'm worried about Anna") or your opinions ("I think Anna may have dyslexia."). Stay with observable actions by your student. At the end of the school year, if Anna's parents are still unwilling to explore Anna's learning strengths and weaknesses, give your notes to your school principal.

Who is eligible to receive services?

To be eligible for special education, children and young people (ages 3–22) must fit into one or more of the following 13 categories, as outlined by IDEA: autism, deaf-blindness, deafness, emotional disturbance, hearing impairment, mental retardation, multiple disabilities, orthopedic impairment, other health impairment, specific learning disability, speech or language impairment, traumatic brain injury, and visual impairment including blindness. Specific definitions of these disabilities vary from state to state. In addition to fitting into one or more of the above listed categories, students must be determined to need special education and related services.

Children between three and nine years of age who are experiencing developmental delays may also be eligible. Infants from birth to age two with developmental delays may be eligible for early intervention help.

What is an eligibility meeting?

At an eligibility meeting, a student is determined to be or not to be eligible to receive special education and related services. A multidisciplinary team meets and discusses the student's formal evaluation, school history, current functioning, test records, and any other relevant data. This team includes the school principal, the special education teacher, and any professionals, such as speech therapists or occupational therapists. The parents are important members of this team, and so are you: the classroom teacher. You are the professional who sees the student every school day in a wide variety of academic and social situations, and your observations are extremely valuable.

Different states have different names for the multidisciplinary teams, such as *pupil placement team*, *eligibility committee*, or *multidisciplinary team*. The exact makeup of the team and the procedures used vary from state to state. Check your state and local regulations for the specifics about this.

What is a least restrictive environment?

If it is determined that your student is eligible for special education services, the term "least restrictive environment" will probably be discussed at the eligibility meeting. This term originates from the concept of special education as a package of instruction and services. Special education is no longer a separate building or separate room where kids with problems are placed when it's decided they need help. "Least restrictive environment" challenges schools to provide an appropriate education for students with disabilities in as "regular" an environment as possible, usually in the same place as kids with no defined disabilities. A student with special needs may spend some time in a resource room for individualized instruction, or he may receive a special form of physical education called Adaptive Physical Education away from the other students, but his home base is the regular classroom. And the goal is to provide as much instruction in the classroom as possible. Sometimes special education teachers and other professionals come into the classroom to provide this instruction.

What happens if my student doesn't qualify for special education?

The multidisciplinary team may have determined that your student fits into one or more of the specific thirteen categories but that he does not need special education services. For example, for the category of specific learning disability, a student, in addition to being defined as having a learning disability, must have a significant discrepancy (1.5 standard deviations) between achievement and potential. Professionals and parents are hotly debating this particular requirement at this time, but as long as it is the law, you could have a student with learning disabilities who is not eligible to receive special education services under IDEA.

He may, however, be eligible for some services under Section 504 of the Rehabilitation Act of 1973 and the Americans with Disabilities Act of 1990. Under these laws, your student may be eligible for accommodations such as preferential seating, the use of a word processor for homework or classwork, the use of a tape recorder in class, more time for writing assignments, and being tested in a different way (for example, orally instead of in written form). These laws offer students with disabilities who are not eligible for services under IDEA a wide range of possible accommodations that can help them quite a bit.

Individualized Education Plans (IEPs)

What is an IEP?

IEP stands for Individualized Education Program. It is a legal document that is developed at an IEP meeting, once it has been determined that a student is eligible for special education services. IDEA established that you are an important member of the IEP meeting.

The IEP document can take different forms in different places. The forms vary from state to state and, in some instances they even differ from county to county or town to town. However, all IEPs must have six different sections. These are:

A **narrative description** of how the student is currently functioning.

Goals and Objectives that describe the desired outcome of the special education services the student will receive.

A **description of any related service** that is needed, such as counseling, speech and language therapy, or special transportation.

A **statement about where the student will receive special services**, such as in the regular classroom or in a resource room or special school.

A **statement about how many hours** the student will receive a given service every week, when this service will start, and for how long it will continue. The **name of the professional** who will provide this service is also included.

A **plan for evaluating** whether or not the student is making progress and how much progress she is making.

At the IEP meeting, you will be asked to sign the front page of the IEP to indicate that you attended the meeting. Prior to this meeting, you may be asked to write a short narrative or fill out a questionnaire that you will bring to the meeting. This will be used to help develop the IEP, especially the section that outlines the student's current functioning in your classroom.

Usually, the professionals who are providing the service write the IEP. For example, if a special education teacher is going to provide five hours of reading instruction a week, she will write out the goals and objectives for that work. If speech services are needed, the speech and language clinician will be asked to write out the goals and objectives for that section. It's a good idea for you to read the IEP once it is written and to ask about any areas of confusion you may have. The best educational program is one in which all the adults working with the student are coordinating efforts and complementing each other's work.

What is an IEP goal? What is an IEP objective? How are they different from each other?

An IEP goal states what is needed. For example, if a student named Sarah were having difficulty with writing skills, she might have the following goal:

> Sarah will independently write paragraphs with at least five sentences in her classroom by June 15.

Objectives state how this goal will be accomplished. For example, for Sarah's writing goal, four objectives could be:

> Sarah will write introductory sentences for paragraphs with a teacher's support by October 15.
>
> Sarah will write introductory sentences for paragraphs independently in her classroom by October 30.
>
> Sarah will write supporting sentences for paragraphs with a teacher's support by November 30.
>
> Sarah will write supporting sentences for paragraphs independently in her classroom by the end of December.

There are two important things to remember about IEP goals and objectives. They should be measurable, so that everyone can agree whether or not they have been achieved. A goal like the following one is too vague:

> Sarah will get better at remembering her multiplication tables.

People could disagree as to whether Sarah has, in fact, achieved this goal. Also, IEP goals and objectives should be clear and easy to understand. If any of them are vague and unclear, or if you don't understand one or more of them, speak with the people who wrote them until you know what is intended.

How should I approach all the reports?

If you have a student who has undergone extensive evaluations, or if you have a student who has received ongoing services in the past, you can be faced with a daunting file. It is important to be aware of your student's learning style and past educational history, but if the file seems too complex, you may feel overwhelmed and unsure of your ability to meet your student's needs. These suggestions may help.

1. Look through the whole file and just see what's there. You can even make a list of the different reports, noting the dates when they were written. Some may be reevaluations of the same skill area—for example, two different reports on speech and language functioning. Prioritize the types of reports that you will read. For example, if your student is experiencing difficulty with social interactions, you may choose to start with the psychological report.

2. Start with the latest reports. Although older reports can contain valuable information, it's easiest to start learning what has been happening more recently. If there is language on a report that interferes with your understanding, ask either the person who wrote the report or another professional what was meant.

3. Note summary statements. Some reports contain extensive and detailed reporting. This is sometimes necessary to establish eligibility for special education and to establish a baseline for future evaluations. For your purposes, however, it's important to know the general information and the conclusions that the evaluator has reached. You don't need to know all the details, especially not when you are first approaching the reports. The summary statements will put the details into perspective and will, in fact, help you understand them more. Lastly, pay special attention to the recommendations made in the reports. If your student is not receiving services that are recommended, you may need to ask your principal or the special education teacher about this.

What is my responsibility regarding my student's IEP goals and objectives?

The special education teacher and other professionals who are responsible for providing instruction as written in the IEP must focus directly on your student's goals and objectives. You also need to be aware of them and to keep them in mind as you teach. For example, Helen Brier's third-grade student Adam, a boy with learning disabilities, was highly interested in the class science project: planting narcissus bulbs and studying their growth cycle. When Helen checked Adam's IEP, she realized that he had a math goal. One of his objectives was to learn how to measure in inches. Another objective was to be able to create a simple chart. Perfect! Every day, Helen asked Adam to measure how high the bulb he'd planted had grown. Then she showed him how to start creating a simple chart. The wonderful thing was that all the kids became interested in measuring and charting, and pretty soon, this became a regular part of the unit.

In addition to special instruction, what other kinds of services can be provided for students with special needs?

A wide range of services can be provided. With the advent of new technology, there are more and more assistive devices that can be helpful, such as communication boards for students who can't speak. Services such as school health services, physical therapy, and counseling for students are available. Parents can receive counseling about the special needs of their child and can be referred to outside resources for support and help. In addition, kids with special needs can participate in therapeutic recreational programs at school and/or in the community. All transportation is provided.

Do students with special needs take standardized tests with the rest of the class?

The multidisciplinary team makes this determination. If modifications are recommended, they are written into the student's IEP. Some students are exempt from standardized tests. Others, such as those with learning disabilities, can be given more time to take the tests, like time and a half, or they can be given the tests untimed. Also, the tests can sometimes be administered in different ways. They might be administered orally, for example, for a student who has significant low vision or blindness.

How can I coordinate my classroom program with the special education teacher and other specialists, like speech therapists?

The most important thing to remember is that it is everyone's job to coordinate efforts. Specialists do sometimes need to focus on providing specific instruction to your student, and you need to help support this. If, for example, there are changes in your class schedule such as field trips or special programs like a school assembly, you need to tell your colleagues about these changes as soon as possible so they can modify their lesson plans for their work with your student.

Specialists also need to focus on supporting your student in his classroom environment. Respectful and honest communication is the key. If you are confused about what a particular specialist is doing and what she needs from you, ask. If you are concerned that an aspect of your student's individualized instruction is interfering with your classroom environment, talk with the specialist about it. Elton Thompson's fifth-grade student Harry receives speech therapy for an expressive language disorder. The only time the speech therapist can come to work with Harry is during silent reading time. They work at the back of the room, but Elton can still hear them working as he sits reading at his desk. If he can hear them in the front of the room, all the kids can hear them.

Elton worries that the noise may distract his student Mary, who has ADD. Elton is also concerned about Harry's privacy. Some of the things that the speech therapist asks Harry to do seem childish even though they are what he needs to work on.

Elton made an appointment with the speech therapist, and together they worked on a solution. The silent reading time needed to stay the same, and the speech therapist had no flexibility with scheduling. There were no private rooms available, so she and Harry needed to stay in the classroom.

The speech therapist suggested that they put up a soundboard that would absorb some of the sound in the far back corner of the classroom. Elton knew playing soft classical music actually helped kids to be more focused. He brought in some Mozart tapes and played them during silent reading. Then he and the speech therapist talked with the kids about how they liked the new system.

Mary asked if she could wear a headset to listen to the classical music. Elton agreed. Harry said that he liked it a whole lot better because now he wasn't afraid all the time that the other kids could hear him.

Do I have to change my classroom rules and procedures for my student with special needs?

Good classroom rules and procedures help everyone: kids with defined special needs and kids with no defined special needs. Most students feel comfortable and are successful in calm, happy classrooms with predictable routines. You do not have to change your good rules and procedures.

Kids with special needs *can* challenge some of your habits. For example, Deborah Russell had gotten used to giving complete and complex directions for any new project to her sixth-grade class. She felt it was better that way because then the kids would understand everything that was expected of them. When she learned, however, that her student Tony, who had a receptive language disorder, could only remember a limited amount of verbal information, she was asked to break down her directions to the class and not to give any more than two directions at a time.

Deborah asked the special education team if it would be all right if she still gave an overview of the project for those students who seemed to like it. The team said, "Sure, as long as you tell them that this is an overview. Say that you will tell them what they need to start doing when you finish."

Deborah experimented. She labeled her overview. She told the class when it was finished. Then, she told them the first thing they needed to do. The thing that surprised her was that no one seemed confused. Tony was happily working, and so was everyone else. Usually, when she finished her long list of directions, she had two or three kids who sat looking out the window. This new way worked better for everyone.

Richard MacKay encouraged creativity in his third graders by having an art area filled with a wide variety of materials. The materials grew until they often spilled into other work areas. Richard's student Althea, who had dyslexia, needed an uncluttered, calm physical environment. She was unable to concentrate on her work when there were crayons and pieces of pretty fabric almost within reach of her desk—if she leaned way over in her chair.

One day when Althea fell reaching for a particularly nice colored pencil (she was scared but not physically hurt), Richard knew he had to make a modification of the physical environment. He still wanted the art supplies readily available, but something had to change. His wife suggested the solution that night at supper. Richard brought in five milk crates and taught the kids how to use them. When they finished working with their supplies, they took their projects to their desks and placed the extra supplies in the crates. These were placed behind the desk: instant neatness.

What if my student with special needs is disrupting my classroom with negative behavior?

If you have tried all the disciplinary techniques that you know about, and your student is still unable to act as a positive member of your classroom community, seek help from the special education team. They are there to help you.

You may need to do things differently for your particular student. For example, many students with mental retardation respond very well to praise. If they are acting inappropriately, it is important to tell them to stop and to tell them what to do instead, without excessive explanations. Then, praise the appropriate behavior. For a student with a nonverbal learning disability, it is usually helpful to explain to them exactly what they are doing that is inappropriate and why this is so. Explain and model a new, better behavior. In this case, a lot of talk helps.

Some kids with special needs require some modifications of the way you interact with them regarding discipline. Your special education team can give you information about this.

If a student continues to exhibit negative behavior, report this to the special education team. It is not just your problem: it is the team's problem, and the team needs to work to find a good solution.

There are regulations in IDEA about serious disciplinary issues. If negative behavior is a result of the student's disability, he cannot be suspended long-term or expelled, and schools are required to develop positive behavior interventions. If a student brings a dangerous weapon to school or has drugs or controlled substances in his possession (and/or tries to sell them), the student may be removed to an alternative educational placement for up to 45 days. Also, if keeping a student in a current placement may result in injury to him or others, he may be removed to an alternative educational placement for up to 45 days.

What if my student receiving special services is still experiencing academic difficulty in my classroom?

Bring this concern to the special education team. It will be most helpful if you first carefully watch for a while and jot down notes about where you see your student not being successful. For example, is he always quiet and never participating in class discussions? Does he talk too much, giving too many details and making the other kids impatient because he's dominating the discussion? Also, bring samples of his work. Nothing speaks so loudly as a student's attempt and failure with a class assignment or a class test.

Things may need to be changed. Cathy Anderson's fourth-grade student Peter, who has Tourette Syndrome, was so successful with spelling tests in third grade that no mention of them was made on his IEP. In fourth grade, however, Peter started tensing up so frequently that his coughing tic became constant. His cough irritated others, which made him even more tense, and he experienced only failure during testing. The team suggested giving Peter his spelling test in a private space so that he could cough and release his tic when he needed to without bothering the other kids (which had made him even more tense). This accommodation was so successful that it was added as a modification on his IEP.

The IEP is a guide. It can and should be changed if it doesn't work for a student. For students with Traumatic Brain Injury, especially, IEPs may need to be changed frequently.

What should I do if my student with special needs is having difficulty relating to other kids and/or is being teased?

Talk with your special education team to find out if there are any unique aspects of your student's disability that make it difficult for him to relate to others. For example, students who have Asperger's Syndrome often simply don't understand the social rules. Usually, knowing this will help you learn what to do for this student, but if you are still feeling unsuccessful after several tries, report the situation to the team. Your student may need counseling services and/or direct instruction about how to relate to others.

Regarding teasing, it is important to make it clear that no teasing or bullying is allowed in your classroom. If a particular student continues to tease or bully, talk with him in a private space and ask him about his behavior. He will sometimes express feelings of anger and resentment toward your student with special needs. Listen to him and acknowledge that he has a right to his feelings. He is, however, not allowed to express them in a negative way. Very specific and clearly stated consequences will follow.

What happens if a parent is not comfortable with a student's progress?

Talk with the parents about their concerns and try to get specifics from them. What is it exactly that they are worried about? Are they concerned about a general lack of progress, or are there specific academic areas that seem more problematic than others? Does their child seem unhappy at school?

Ask the parents if they would like to meet with the special education team or if they would prefer that you report their concerns. Parents are important members of your student's team, and they often have valuable information that can inform what should happen at school.

What should I do if I'm not comfortable with a student's progress?

First, take some time to carefully observe your student in various settings. Jot down informal notes so that you can figure out what is making you uncomfortable. Are you having a vague, general feeling, or can you see specific situations where your student is acting in an unhappy or inappropriate way? *Where* is he being unsuccessful? *What* is he being unsuccessful with? Once you really know the cause of your discomfort, talk with the special education team and tell them your concerns. Serving a student with special needs is an ongoing process that may require many modifications.

How do I know if I'm doing a good job?

First, distinguish between a good job and a perfect job. Nobody does a perfect job. All teachers make mistakes at times, and it is important that you recognize your mistakes, acknowledge them, learn from them, and go on. Some of the finest teachers are people who constantly critique their own effectiveness. They see where they need some work, and they ask for help in these areas. They also notice the places where they are successful, and they appreciate themselves for that.

You may be truly concerned about whether or not you are doing a good job with your student with special needs, especially if your student has a significant disability that you have never dealt with before. For example, you may have a student in your classroom who is totally blind. In this case, ask the special education teacher or another trusted person from the team to come in and observe your work. This can feel intimidating, but you will find that most people are very positive with a person who is honestly asking for feedback so that he or she can do a better job for a student. Your desire to do a good job is a key element, and it will be appreciated.

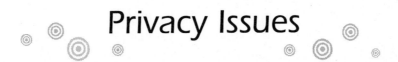

Privacy Issues

What information am I free to divulge to other people, including other professionals, about my student's needs?

Under IDEA, you are allowed to discuss your student's diagnosis and special needs only to those school professionals, including other teachers, who have a need to know in order to provide an appropriate education for your student. You can't talk about your student's diagnosis or needs freely in the teachers' room.

In an emergency health or safety situation, you can give relevant information to an appropriate professional such as a doctor or paramedic. Your school should provide specific guidelines about whom you can talk to and when.

Sometimes, your student may need a special accommodation when a visitor joins your class. Linda Dawson's fifth-grade student Carla who has a significant hearing loss needs to be told all the rules of a game in a quiet space before the game begins. When a person from a local community group came in to teach the kids a cooperative game, Carla still needed this. Linda could tell the visitor about Carla's need for this accommodation, but that is all she could tell her.

Sometimes, you can be caught off-guard. One day, Malcolm Devens received a call from a teacher at a school in a nearby town. His second-grade student Tommy, who has muscular dystrophy, had moved the week before, and the teacher was calling for information. Malcolm declined to provide any information. He told the teacher to check with her special education team to find out the information she needed to know. Malcolm had no way of knowing exactly who was calling. Not offering any information was the right thing.

There are times when it can be important for you to talk with people outside of the school, such as when your student is receiving counseling. In this case, a parent of your student needs to sign a release form before you can have this conversation.

Do I talk with my other students about the special needs of a student in my class? If so, what do I say?

You always need to protect the privacy of your student with special needs. It is against the law to divulge any information to anyone about your student's disability or special needs without consent from the student's family. Sometimes, parents of a student with special needs will ask to come to your class, or to have some other person come to class, to talk with your students about the disability that your student lives with. This can be very helpful. Disabilities like Tourette Syndrome or autism, especially, in which there can be overt inappropriate behaviors, become more understandable and, therefore, less frightening.

The only thing you can discuss with all your students is any overt behavior that occurs in your classroom. This can be positive behavior or negative behavior. In the case of the former, everyone can celebrate success. In the case of the latter, the class can discuss possible solutions.

Appendix
Resources

LEARNING DISABILITIES
Dyslexia, Dyscalcula, and Dysgraphia

Shaywitz, Sally. (2003). *Overcoming Dyslexia: A New and Complete Science-Based Program for Reading Problems at Any Level*, Knopf. Dr. Sally Shaywitz has done immensely valuable research into the causes and nature of dyslexia. In this book, she integrates her work in the lab with practical aspects of teaching people with dyslexia to read.

Stevens, Suzanne H. (1996). *The LD Child and the ADHD Child: Ways Parents and Professionals Can Help*, John F. Blair, Publisher. This very accessible book gives excellent information about the issues that are involved with learning disabilities and ADHD.

Stowe, Cynthia M. (2002). *How to Reach & Teach Children & Teens with Dyslexia: A Parent and Teacher Guide to Helping Students of All Ages Academically, Socially and Emotionally*, Jossey-Bass, 2002. This practical guide gives many suggestions on specific ways to teach people with dyslexia. Through interviews with people who have had personal experience with dyslexia, it also provides a sense of how this learning disability affects people's lives.

West, Thomas G. (1997). *In the Mind's Eye: Visual Thinkers, Gifted People With Dyslexia and Other Learning Difficulties, Computer Images and the Ironies of Creativity*, Prometheus Books. This book brings forth the positive aspects of dyslexia and other forms of less traditional learning styles. It profiles several famous people who are believed to have had a form of dyslexia, such as Winston Churchill and Thomas Edison.

www.interdys.org is the Web site of the International Dyslexia Association.
www.dyslexia-teacher.com is an online magazine about dyslexia.
www.ldonline.org offers a lot of accessible information on learning disabilities in general.

Nonverbal Learning Disabilities

Tanguay, Pamela B. and Sue Thompson. (2002). *Nonverbal Learning Disabilities at School: Educating Students with NLD, Asperger Syndrome and Related Conditions*, Jessica Kingsley Publishers. This practical guide offers many good suggestions on how to work with people with NLD and related disorders.

Thompson, Sue. (1997). *The Source for Nonverbal Learning Disorders*, LinguiSystems. This book was first self-published with the title *I Shouldn't Have to Tell You*. It is a pioneering work that disseminates accurate and helpful information about the disorder.

www.nldline.com is a Web site devoted to educating people about nonverbal learning disabilities.
www.nldontheweb.org offers valuable information about nonverbal learning disabilities.
www.NLDA.org is the Web site for the national Nonverbal Learning Disability Association.

TRAUMATIC BRAIN INJURY

D'Amato, Rik, Elaine Clark, and Robert Diamond. (1998). "Traumatic Brain Injury (TBI), A Handout for Teachers." In S. Canter and Servio A. Carroll (Eds.), *Helping Children at Home and School: Handouts From Your School Psychologist*, (pp. 617–620). National Association of School Psychologists. This concise four-page handout gives a definition of the problem, an overview of the issues, suggestions for how teachers can help, and a short listing of resources.

Lash, Marilyn. (1992). *When Your Child Goes to School After an Injury*, Exceptional Parent. This excellent pamphlet gives good explanations of important issues and excellent guidance in how to help a child re-enter school.

Moore, Adam. (1990). *Broken Arrow Boy*, Landmark Editions. At the age of 8, Adam fell onto an arrow and suffered a head injury. He wrote this book at age 9. It is a wonderful book, full of honesty and humor. (This book was a Gold Award Winner in the 1989 National Awards Contest for Students.)

www.biausa.org is the Web site of the Brain Injury Association. Click on "For Kids & Parents" and then "Treatment & Rehabilitation" and then on "Returning to Work & School."

ADD and ADHD

Flick, Grad L. (2002). *ADD/ADHD Behavior-Change Resource Kit: Ready-to-Use Strategies and Activities for Helping Children With Attention Deficit Disorder*, Jossey-Bass. This comprehensive book gives a great deal of background information on attention issues, as well as practical suggestions for parents, teachers, and mental health professionals.

Rief, Sandra. F. (1993). *How to Reach and Teach ADD/ADHD Children: Practical Techniques, Strategies, and Interventions for Helping Children With Attention Problems and Hyperactivity*, Jossey-Bass. This classic book is filled with ways to help kids with attention issues succeed in school.

Rief, Sandra. F. (2002). *The ADD/ADHD Checklist: An Easy Reference for Parents & Teachers*, Jossey-Bass. This book presents basic information about ADD and ADHD in checklist form for both teachers and parents. It is full of helpful tips.

A.D.D. Warehouse, at **www.addwarehouse.com** or 800-233-9273, is a company that offers many books and other resources about ADD/ADHD.
www.chadd.org is the Web site for Children and Adults with Attention Deficit/Hyperactivity Disorder (CHADD).

Autism

Grandin, Temple. (1996). *Thinking in Pictures: And Other Reports From My Life With Autism*, Vintage. Dr. Grandin, who has autism, has written a clear and honest book about life with autism. Grandin is high functioning, yet her autism has shaped her life. This book is extremely helpful for anyone who truly wants to understand autism.

www.autism-society.org is the Web site of the Autism Society of America.
www.autism.org is the Web site of the Center for the Study of Autism.
www.autism.org/temple/ inside.html presents the article "An Inside View of Autism" by Temple Grandin, Ph.D., Assistant Professor, Colorado State University.

Asperger's Syndrome

Bashe, Patricia Romanowski and Barbara L. Kirby. (2001). *The OASIS Guide to Asperger Syndrome: Advice, Support, Insight, and Inspiration*, Crown. This book is practical, accessible, and warm. Written by two parents of kids with Asperger Syndrome, it presents valuable information but doesn't overwhelm with extensive medical or educational jargon.

Faherty, Catherine. (2000). *Asperger's: What Does It Mean To Me?* Future Horizons. This workbook is geared to the student with Asperger's Syndrome.

www.udel.edu/bkirby/asperger/as whatisit.html is a short online article by Barbara L. Kirby that provides good insight into Asperger's Syndrome.
www.aspergersyndrome.org is the Web site for O.A.S.I.S., the Online Asperger Syndrome Information and Support group.

Tourette Syndrome

Byalick, Marcia. (2002). *Quit It*, Delacorte Books for Young Readers. This sensitive book tells the story of Carrie, a seventh-grade girl who has been newly diagnosed with Tourette Syndrome (TS) While life is sometimes hard for Carrie because of her tics, this is a hopeful book. TS is only a part of Carrie's life. The book is written for 9- to 12-year-olds.

www.tsa-usa.org is the Web site of the Tourette Syndrome Association, Inc. "*Tourette Syndrome: An Inside Perspective*" (2002) is a great article written by Susan Conners, a woman who has Tourette Syndrome. It is on the National Association of School Psychologists web site, **www.nasponline.org/pub lications/cq312tsconnors.html**.

Mental Retardation

Weber, Jayne Dixon (Ed.). (2000). *Children with Fragile X Syndrome: A Parents' Guide*, Woodbine House. This book explains this often misunderstood disability very well.

www.ndss.org is the Web site for the National Down Syndrome Society. There is an excellent article on this site called "The Educational Challenges Inclusion Study." To find this article, click on "Information & Resources," then click on "Education & Schooling," then click on "Inclusion Study," and finally, click on "full text of the study report."
www.thearc.org is the Web site of the Association of Retarded Citizens (Arc) of the United States.

GIFTED AND TALENTED

Galbraith, Judy and Delisle, Jim. (1996). *The Gifted Kid's Survival Guide: A Teen Handbook*, Free Spirit Publishing. This book addresses many of the issues that gifted kids deal with. It's a friendly, effective book.

www.aagc.org is the Web site of the American Association for Gifted Children at Duke University.
www.jhu.edu/gifted is the Web site for the Center for Talented Youth, John Hopkins University.
www.nagc.org is the Web site for the National Association for Gifted Children (NAGC).

PARTIAL HEARING LOSS AND DEAFNESS

Clemente, Gary. (1994). *Cosmo Gets an Ear*, Modern Signs Press. This picture book for kids tells the story of Cosmo, a boy who has to get a hearing aid.

Yates, Elizabeth. (1987). *Sound Friendships: The Story of Willa and Her Hearing Ear Dog*, Countryman Press. Willa lost her hearing at age 14, when a firecracker exploded next to her ear. This book tells the story of how, as a young woman, she received a hearing-ear dog, and how this wonderful gift changed her life.

www.hearingloss.org is an advocacy Web site for people with hearing loss.
www.agbell.org is the Web site for the Alexander Graham Bell Association for the Deaf and Hard of Hearing.
www.asha.org is the Web site for the American Speech-Language-Hearing Association.

LOW VISION AND BLINDNESS

Torres, Iris and Anne L. Corn. (1990). *When You Have a Visually Handicapped Child in Your Classroom: Suggestions for Teachers*, American Foundation for the Blind, New York. This extremely helpful pamphlet is filled with practical suggestions.

www.afb.org is the Web site for the American Foundation for the Blind.
www.acb.org is the Web site for the American Council of the Blind.
www.rfbd.org is the Web site for Recording for the Blind and Dyslexic.

SPEECH AND LANGUAGE DISORDERS

Hamaguchi, Patricia McAleer. (2001). *Childhood Speech, Language & Listening Problems, 2nd Edition*, John Wiley and Sons. Primarily written for parents, this book offers clear information on the development of speech and language and the difficulties that sometimes occur. It is a friendly and accessible book.

www.asha.org is the Web site for the American Speech-Language-Hearing Association.
www.stutteringhelp.org is the Web site for the Stuttering Foundation of America. They produce a catalogue filled with books and videos and other resources about stuttering. They also will send free brochures, including, "The Child Who Stutters at School: Notes to the Teacher." A 20-minute video and booklet called, "Stuttering: Straight Talk for Teachers" can be purchased for a modest price. Their phone number is 800-992-9392.

PHYSICAL DISABILITIES AND HEALTH IMPAIRMENTS

Bergman, Thomas. (1989). *On Our Own Terms, Children Living With Physical Handicaps*, Gareth Stevens Publishing. This picture book is appropriate for more than just young children. It shows large photographs of real children dealing with physical challenges. The text is simple but still portrays the challenges and triumphs associated with physical disabilities.

EMOTIONAL DISTURBANCE AND BEHAVIORAL DISORDERS

Krementz, Jill. (1984). *How It Feels When Parents Divorce*, Knopf. In this book, 19 different kids, aged seven to sixteen, tell the story of their parents' divorce. Each story starts with a full-page photo of the child, and these add to the poignant and effective narratives.

www.nimh.nih.gov is the Web site for the National Institute of Mental Health.
www.nmha.org is the Web site for the National Mental Health Association.

GOOD GENERAL RESOURCES

Anderson, Winifred, Stephen Chitwood, and Deidre Hayden. (1997). *Negotiating the Special Education Maze: A Guide for Parents & Teachers*, Woodbine House. This book is a great guide to the system of special education for both parents and teachers. It's clear and easy to understand.

Greene, Lawrence J. (1998). *Finding Help When Your Child Is Struggling in School: From Kindergarten Through Junior High School*, Golden Books. This resource focuses on meeting a child's needs in the special education system. There is excellent information about evaluations and the professionals who provide services.

Hammeken, Peggy A. (2000). *Inclusion: 450 Strategies for Success: A Practical Guide for All Educators Who Teach Students With Disabilities*, Peytral Publications. This book is chock-full of suggestions for teaching kids with special needs in the major academic areas. It also deals with organizational skills, giving directions, and large-group instruction. Twenty-five helpful worksheets are provided.

Koplewicz, Harold S. (1997) *It's Nobody's Fault: New Hope and Help for Difficult Children and Their Parents*, Three Rivers Press. This book gives helpful information about many conditions that are organically based.

Shore, Kenneth. (1994). *The Parents' Public School Handbook: How to Make the Most of Your Child's Education, from Kindergarten Through Middle School*, Simon & Schuster. Meant for parents, this book provides information on a wide variety of topics, from parent-teacher relationships to music instruction.

www.nichcy.org is the Web site of the National Dissemination Center for Children with Disabilities (NICHCY). This organization focuses on helping teachers work with students with disabilities. You can e-mail them with specific questions at **nichcy@aed.org**, or call at 800-695-0285.

ORGANIZATIONS
Asthma and Allergy
Asthma and Allergy Foundation of America
800-727-8462
www.aafa.org

Birth Defects
March of Dimes Birth Defects Foundation
914-428-7100
www.marchofdimes.com (English)
www.nacersano.org (Spanish)
(Go to the Web site to obtain basic information. You can e-mail them at **askus@marchofdimes.com** with specific questions.)

Burns
Phoenix Society for Burn Survivors
800-888-2876
www.phoenix-society.org

Cerebral Palsy
United Cerebral Palsy
800-872-5827
www.ucp.org

Cystic Fibrosis
Cystic Fibrosis Foundation
800-344-4823
www.cff.org
(You can search for your closest CF Care Center on the Web site. A Care Center can provide you with the information you need.)

Diabetes
Juvenile Diabetes Research Foundation
800-533-2873
www.jdrf.org

Epilepsy
Epilepsy Foundation
800-332-1000
www.epilepsyfoundation.org

Multiple Sclerosis
National Multiple Sclerosis Society
800-344-4867
www.nationalmssociety.org

Muscular Dystrophy
Muscular Dystrophy Association
800-572-1717
www.mdausa.org

Rare Disorders
National Organization for Rare Disorders
800-999-6673
www.rarediseases.org

Spina Bifida
Spina Bifida Association of America
800-621-3141
www.sbaa.org

National Health Information Center (NHIC)
800-336-4797
www.health.gov/nhic
This is a place where you can go to get a referral to a national organization. They do not provide information on any particular health issue, but they tell you where you can seek this information.